MW01671333

Christ IN ALL OF *Scripture*

VOL. 2

THIS STUDY BELONGS TO:

THE DAILY GRACE CO.®

Christ in All of Scripture: A 52-Week Journey of Discovering Jesus on Every Page of the Bible | Volume 2

The Daily Grace Co.® exists to equip disciples to know and love God and His Word by creating beautiful, theologically rich, and accessible resources so that God may be glorified and the gospel made known.

Designed in the United States of America and printed in China.

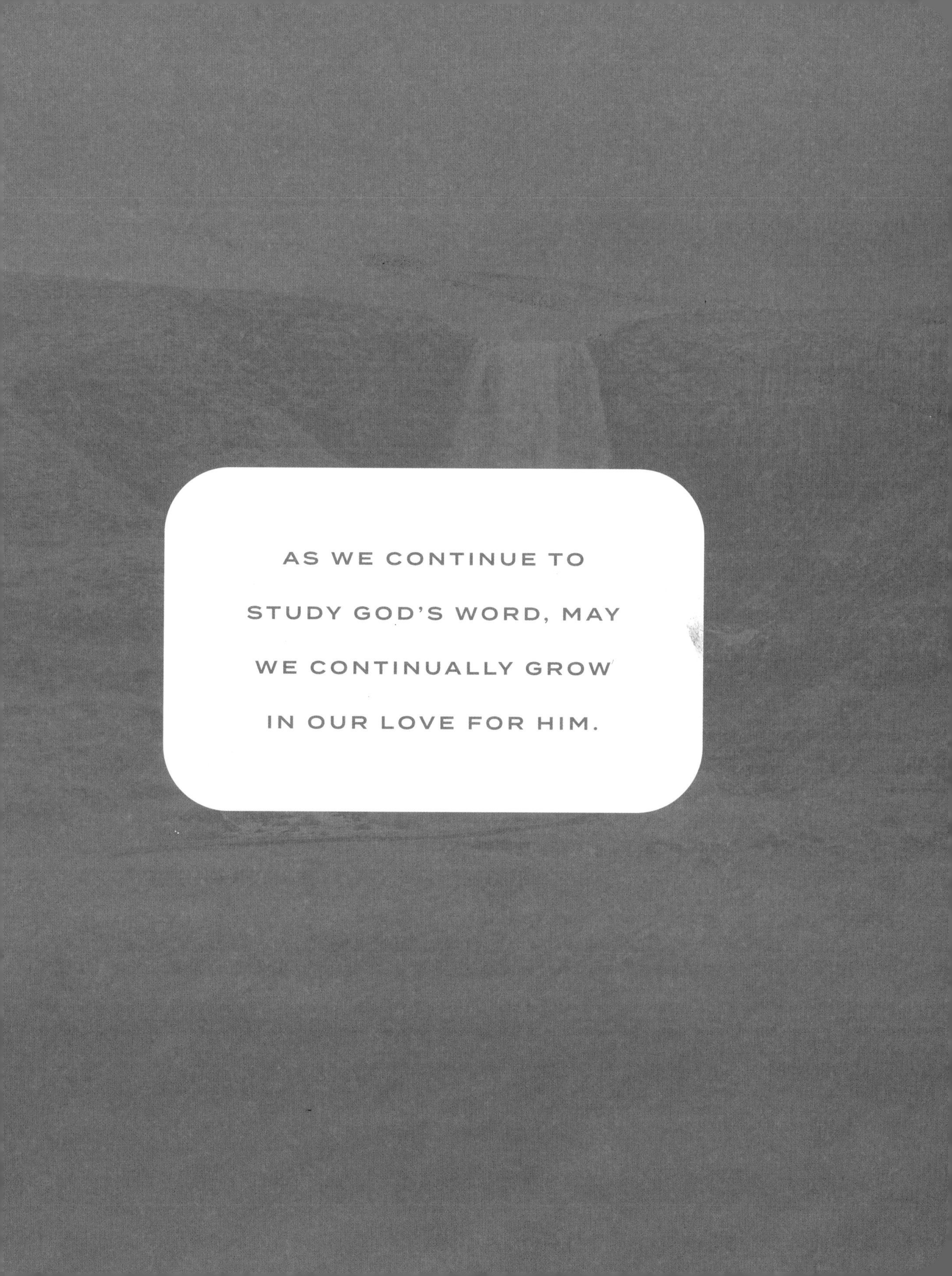

AS WE CONTINUE TO
STUDY GOD'S WORD, MAY
WE CONTINUALLY GROW
IN OUR LOVE FOR HIM.

TABLE OF CONTENTS

INTRODUCTION TO
Christ in All of Scripture

Welcome to *Christ in All of Scripture: A 52-Week Journey of Discovering Jesus on Every Page of the Bible | Volume 2*!

As you continue in your study, remember that the Old Testament and New Testament tell one story, and they are far more intertwined than we sometimes realize. As we saw from the beginning of the first volume, that story begins in the Old Testament, and it contains numerous threads that run throughout and find their resolution in the New Testament. Because of this, we cannot fully appreciate the New Testament without also appreciating the Old—and vice versa.

And standing at the center of this one story that unites both testaments is Jesus Christ. He Himself is the main character and climax of the story begun in the Old Testament. For that reason, we can appropriately say that Jesus Christ is present in all of Scripture, not just a quarter of it.

Of course, it's easy to say that Jesus is in all of Scripture. But the study you hold in your hands will help you see it. And our prayer is that in seeing how He is present throughout the whole Bible, your love for Jesus and for His Word will grow.

HOW TO USE THIS RESOURCE

As our journey continues, this section provides reminders of some practical considerations that will help you make the most of this study.

In This Study

This study is the second of four volumes in the *Christ in All of Scripture* study set from The Daily Grace Co. Each volume covers roughly one quarter, or thirteen weeks, of content. And together, these four volumes were designed to be completed over the course of one calendar year—from January 1 through December 31.

Over the course of this year—just as we did in the first volume—we will continue walking through passages from most of the books of the Old Testament, showing how these passages ultimately point to Jesus. In this way, we will discover how Christ is truly present on every page and in every passage of Scripture.

Weekly Rhythms

The main content of this volume starts in Week 14. There are five days of content for each week, so most readers will likely find it helpful to complete the study content on Mondays through Fridays. Then, the weekends can be used to catch up on any missed study days or to reflect on what you learned.

Each week in this volume contains the following elements:

WEEKLY INTRODUCTION

Each week will begin with a short introduction that will share the two passages of Scripture we will study that week—one from the Old Testament and one from the New Testament.

DAYS 1 AND 3: "MARK IT UP"

On Days 1 and 3, you will be asked to repetitively read and annotate our two weekly passages. If the idea of annotation seems overwhelming to you—perhaps something you have not done since high school English class—do not fret! We will provide helpful prompts to guide you along the way. You can also find some annotation examples on pages 201–206.

These study days might initially seem quite short, especially compared to past Bible studies you may have completed, but we encourage you to make the most of this step! The observations you make on Days 1 and 3—through the highlights, underlines, and notes you write in the margins—will guide the rest of your progress throughout the week.

Additionally, if you come across a prompt that challenges you or leaves you with more questions than answers, that's okay! You may find it helpful to look at the surrounding context of that passage (i.e., the verses or chapters that come just before and just after it). And at times, you may simply jot down your questions to come back to later in the week.

For annotation examples, as well as other helpful tips and tools for completing this study, see the Appendix, starting on page 195.

HOW TO USE THIS RESOURCE

DAYS 2 AND 4: "GO DEEPER" + "MAKE THE CHRIST CONNECTION"
On Days 2 and 4, you will find commentary that helps further explain and connect that week's passages of Scripture, as well as some questions that will help you more deeply consider what you have read and make connections of your own. We suggest you begin these days by rereading the passages. Then, give yourself plenty of time to read the commentary and answer the questions as you go deeper into each passage.

DAY 5: "LIVE IT OUT"
Finally, the week will end with some intentional time to consider how you might apply what you have learned. This is an important step that will help you move from head knowledge to heart knowledge and then to actionable steps to live out the truths you have learned. We suggest you start Day 5 by reading that week's two main passages of Scripture once more and then setting aside some time to pray and walk through the provided application questions as you consider how God might be calling you to respond.

Whether this is your first time completing a Bible study or you have been studying God's Word for decades, the unique weekly format of this study may still feel new and perhaps even challenging at first. If that's the case for you, don't forget to give yourself grace through the process and remember that God has not left you to study His Word on your own. If you are a believer, His Spirit dwells within you and will guide you as you approach Scripture.

As You Continue

Ready to keep going? As you continue in this yearlong journey, remember that the goal of this study is not perfection but growth in your understanding of God's Word. In other words, we do not expect you to annotate every passage or answer every question perfectly. Instead—day by day, week by week, and volume by volume—we pray that you would progressively grow in your ability to see Christ in all of Scripture. And as you do, we pray that you will grow to love Him and His Word more.

Jesus is the main character of the story. He is the One to whom all of Scripture points. And so, let us seek to magnify Him as we embark on the remaining weeks of study. To Him be the glory!

Visit www.thedailygraceco.com to purchase the other three volumes in this study set (Volumes 1, 3, and 4).

STUDY SUGGESTIONS

We believe that the Bible is true, trustworthy, and timeless and that it is vitally important for all believers. These study suggestions are intended to help you more effectively study Scripture as you seek to know and love God through His Word.

SUGGESTED STUDY TOOLS

- Bible
- Journal to write notes or prayers
- Pens, colored pencils, and highlighters
- Dictionary to look up unfamiliar words

DID YOU KNOW THAT THERE IS A PODCAST THAT GOES ALONG WITH THIS STUDY?

A YEAR IN THE BIBLE

WITH DAILY GRACE®

Check out season 4 of *A Year in the Bible with Daily Grace* for encouragement as you complete this study — available wherever you listen to podcasts.

HOW TO STUDY THE BIBLE

The Inductive Method provides tools for deeper and more intentional Bible study. This study will guide you through the three steps of the Inductive Method listed below—equipping you to observe, interpret, and apply two passages of Scripture each week. In addition, the questions listed under each of the steps below can be used to aid your study of the weekly passages.

Weekly rhythm: *On Days 1 and 3 of each week, we recommend referring to the "observation and comprehension" step and key question. On Days 2 and 4, we recommend following the "interpretation" step and key question. And on Day 5, we recommend referencing the "application" step and key question.*

1 Observation + Comprehension

KEY QUESTION: WHAT DOES THE TEXT SAY?

After reading the daily Scripture in its entirety at least once, begin working with smaller portions of the Scripture. Read a passage of Scripture repetitively, and then mark the following items in the text:

- *Key or repeated words and ideas*
- *Key themes*
- *Transition words (e.g., therefore, but, because, if/then, likewise, etc.)*
- *Lists*
- *Comparisons and contrasts*
- *Commands*
- *Unfamiliar words (look these up in a dictionary)*
- *Questions you have about the text*

2

Interpretation

KEY QUESTION: WHAT DOES THE TEXT MEAN?

Once you have annotated the text, work through the following steps to help you interpret its meaning:

- *Read the passage in other versions for a better understanding of the text.*
- *Read cross-references to help interpret Scripture with Scripture.*
- *Paraphrase or summarize the passage to check for understanding.*
- *Identify how the text reflects the metanarrative of Scripture, which is the story of creation, fall, redemption, and restoration.*
- *Read trustworthy commentaries if you need further insight into the meaning of the passage.*

3

Application

KEY QUESTION: HOW SHOULD THE TRUTH OF THIS PASSAGE CHANGE ME?

Bible study is not merely an intellectual pursuit. The truths about God, ourselves, and the gospel that we discover in Scripture should produce transformation in our hearts and lives. Answer the following questions and prompts as you consider what you have learned in your study:

- *What attributes of God's character are revealed in the passage?*
- *Consider places where the text directly states the character of God, as well as how His character is revealed through His words and actions.*
- *What do I learn about myself in light of who God is?*
- *Consider how you fall short of God's character, how the text reveals your sin nature, and what it says about your new identity in Christ.*
- *How should this truth change me?*
- *A passage of Scripture may contain direct commands telling us what to do or warnings about sins to avoid in order to help us grow in holiness. Other times, our application flows out of seeing ourselves in light of God's character. As we pray and reflect on how God is calling us to change in light of His Word, we should be asking questions like, "How should I pray for God to change my heart?" and "What practical steps can I take toward cultivating habits of holiness?"*

TIMELINE OF SCRIPTURE

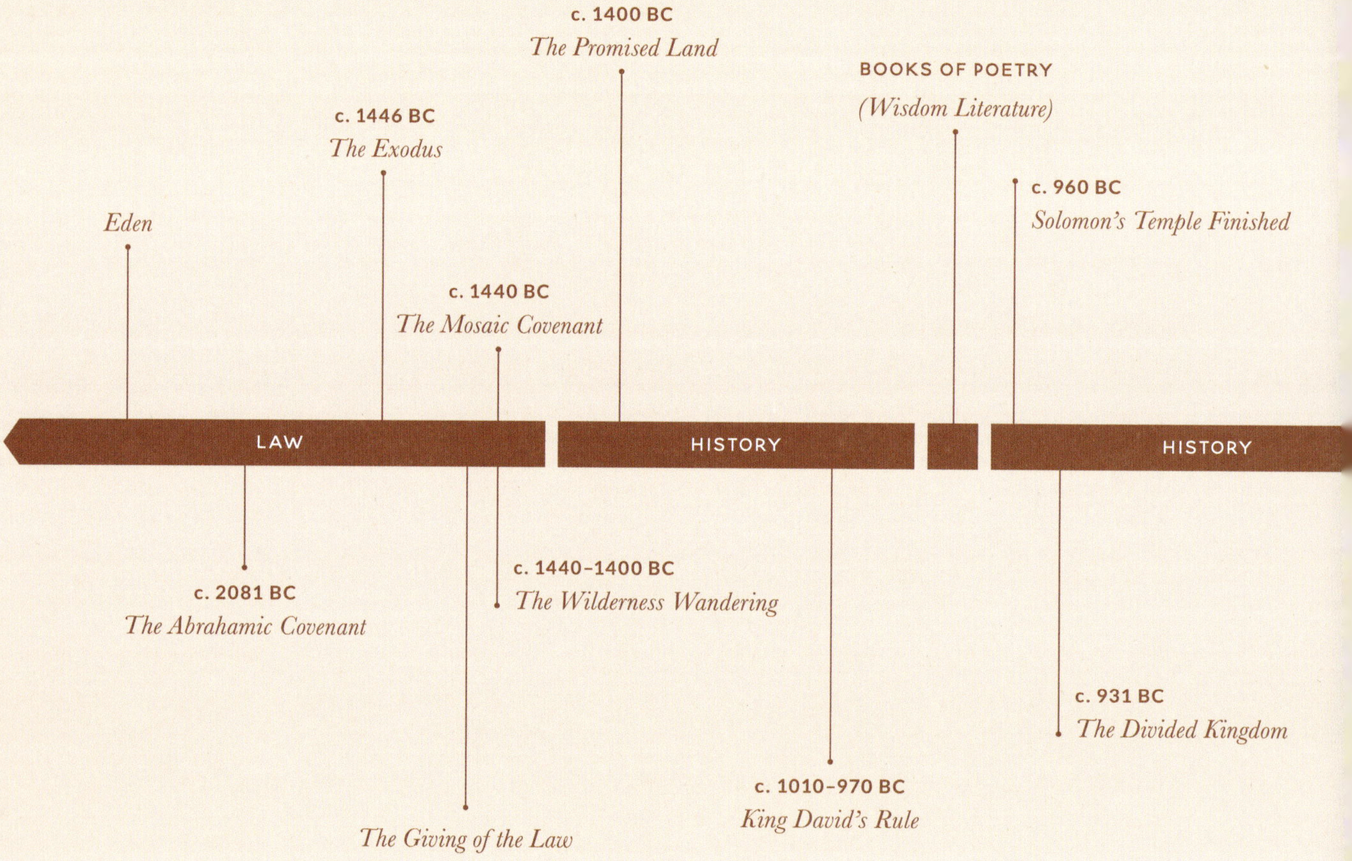

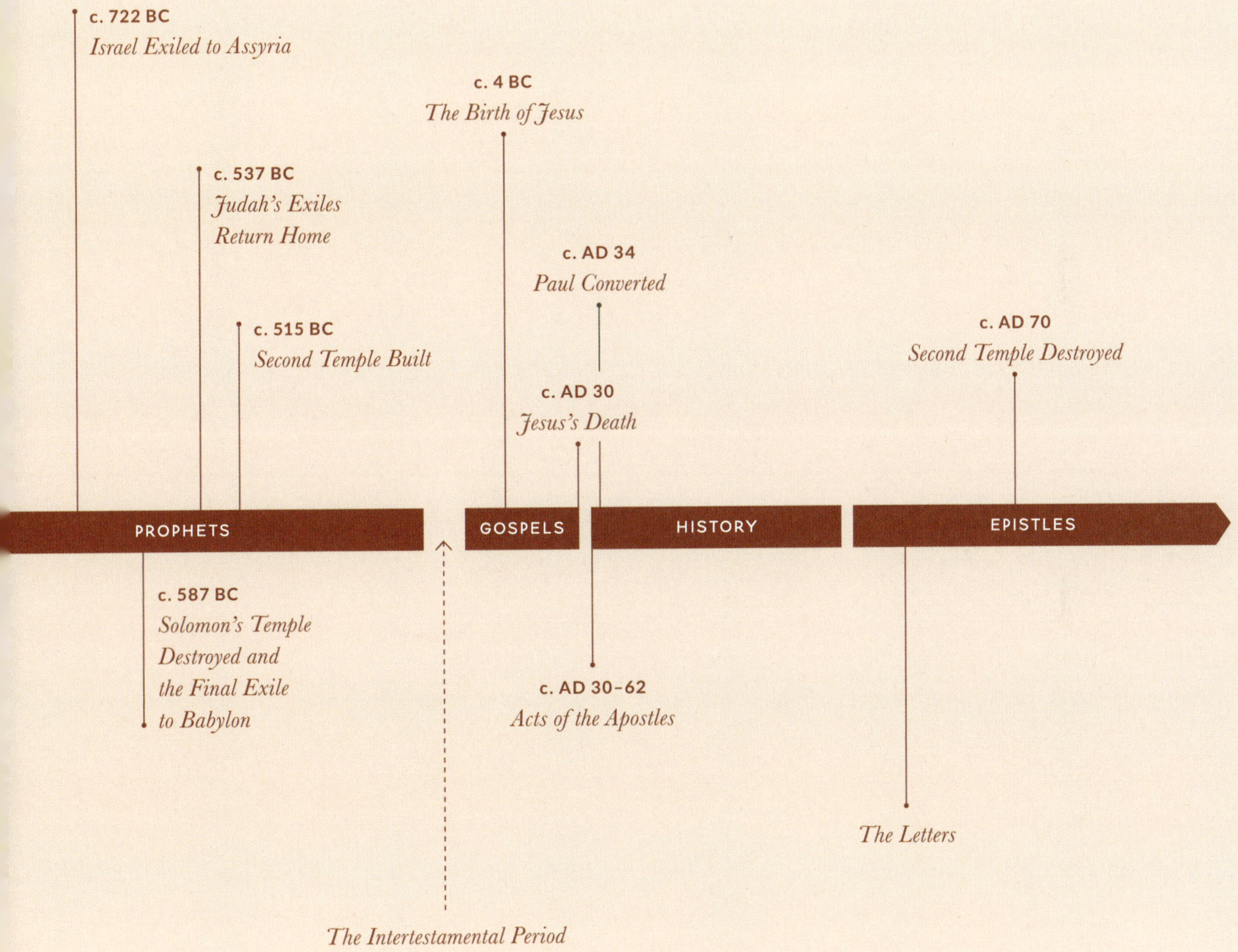
c. 722 BC
Israel Exiled to Assyria
c. 537 BC
Judah's Exiles Return Home
c. 515 BC
Second Temple Built
c. 587 BC
Solomon's Temple Destroyed and the Final Exile to Babylon
PROPHETS
The Intertestamental Period
c. 4 BC
The Birth of Jesus
GOSPELS
c. AD 34
Paul Converted
c. AD 30
Jesus's Death
HISTORY
c. AD 30–62
Acts of the Apostles
c. AD 70
Second Temple Destroyed
EPISTLES
The Letters

Introduction

WEEK FOURTEEN

This week, we will look at God's presence filling the tabernacle in Exodus 40:34–38. We will also examine John 1:10–14 to see how the presence and glory of God came to earth to dwell in human flesh—the body of Jesus Christ. You will learn that you, too, are now the dwelling place of God's Spirit and have access to God's presence.

MARK IT UP

Old Testament Passage

Today, we will begin to study Exodus 40:34–38. In doing so, we will see how the glory of the Lord filled the tabernacle and guided the Israelites through the wilderness. Read the passage two or three times and annotate, or mark up, the text as you read. For tips and examples on annotating, see pages 196–207.

1. Highlight any words or phrases that point to Christ.

2. Make note of any attributes of God seen in the text.

3. Circle all instances of "the cloud." What was this cloud?

4. Underline any references to "the tabernacle."

5. Highlight verse 35. What does this tell you about God's presence?

EXODUS 40:34–38

34 The cloud covered the tent of meeting, and the glory of
the LORD filled the tabernacle. 35 Moses was unable to enter
the tent of meeting because the cloud rested on it, and the
glory of the Lord filled the tabernacle. 36 The Israelites set
out whenever the cloud was taken up from the tabernacle
throughout all the stages of their journey. 37 If the cloud was
not taken up, they did not set out until the day it was taken up.
38 For the cloud of the Lord was over the tabernacle by day, and
there was a fire inside the cloud by night, visible to the entire
house of Israel throughout all the stages of their journey.

Go Deeper

1 Read Exodus 40:34–38.

These verses mark the end of the book of Exodus. As the book comes to a close, we see that God's promises are beginning to be fulfilled.

2 Read Exodus 6:6–7. What was God's promise to the people of Israel?

He has delivered the people from their slavery "with an outstretched arm and great acts of judgment" (Exodus 6:6). Now, He has had them construct a tabernacle—a dwelling place—for Him so that He can live among them as their God and they as His people. The plagues, the Passover lamb, the crossing of the Red Sea, and the construction of the tabernacle with great craft and detail—all of it had been building to this moment. Finally, the presence of God is not outside of the camp on the mountain, but it has come down into the midst of the people. This is indicative of Israel's relationship to God. He is their God, and they are His people.

3 Where else in the Bible is there mention of a beautiful place where God has a perfect relationship with His people?

If you read through the instructions for building the tabernacle in Exodus 25–27 and its construction in Exodus 35–40, you may notice some parallels between these chapters and the first two chapters of the Old Testament. In Genesis 1–2, God carefully and beautifully constructed the earth. He designed it perfectly, ordered it appropriately, and called it good. Similarly, each piece of the tabernacle is intentionally crafted and carefully ordered.

God set apart the garden of Eden—with the Tree of Life at the center—as the place where He walked with and lived in relationship with His people. In the same way, the inner meeting place of the tabernacle is constructed with a tree-like lampstand (Exodus 37:17–22) at the center, and it is there where God's presence will dwell.

God rested at the end of His creation work (Genesis 2:2), and likewise, at the end of Moses's work on the tabernacle, God's presence comes to rest in the tent. This moment in Israel's history is an undoing of the effects of the Fall. Though God's relationship with His people is still not perfectly restored—it requires the remediation of sin through the sacrificial system—it is still a taste of Eden and all its goodness for the Israelites.

4 Read Exodus 6:8. How does this part of God's promise to Israel relate to our passage in Exodus 40:34–38?

By the last chapter of Exodus, God has indeed brought deliverance and has claimed the Israelites as His own people by finally coming to dwell in their midst. However, by looking back on His promise to the people in Exodus 6, we see that there is still one aspect of the promise that has yet to be fulfilled. Exodus ends with rejoicing and relief but also with hopeful expectation. The Israelites are still in the wilderness, but the cloud of God's glory that now dwells among them will be their guide as they continue their journey to their final destination.

MARK IT UP

New Testament Passage

Over the past two days, we have studied how God's glory filled the tabernacle and how He led the Israelites through the wilderness. Now, in today's passage, we will see the same God become flesh in order to dwell among us and restore our relationship with Him. Read John 1:10–14 two or three times and annotate, or mark up, the text as you read. For tips and examples on annotating, see page 196–207.

1. Highlight any words or phrases that point to Christ.

2. Make note of any attributes of God seen in the text.

3. Look back at Exodus 40:34–38. Now, return to John 1:10–14 and underline any connecting words or themes that you see between the two passages.

4. Circle any references to God's people. Who are God's people?

JOHN 1:10–14

10 He was in the world, and the world was created through
him, and yet the world did not recognize him. 11 He came to
his own, and his own people did not receive him. 12 But to all
who did receive him, he gave them the right to be children
of God, to those who believe in his name, 13 who were born,
not of natural descent, or of the will of the flesh, or of the
will of man, but of God. 14 The Word became flesh and
dwelt among us. We observed his glory, the glory as the
one and only Son from the Father, full of grace and truth.

Make the Christ Connection

1 Read Exodus 40:34–38 and John 1:10–14.

"The Word became flesh." In other words, the all-powerful Creator—the One who spoke to bring light out of darkness and bring all creation into existence—became a human being. The same God whose glory filled the tabernacle took on a human body.

2 Read Colossians 1:19. Take a moment and meditate on what it means for the fullness of God to have dwelt in the person of Jesus.

God's plan was always to dwell with His people, but the consequence of the Fall (Genesis 3) was separation from Him. His glory and goodness required perfect obedience, but humanity was now tainted by sin and death. In Exodus 33:18–20, we see that even Moses, the righteous leader and deliverer of the people, could not see the full glory of God without the risk of death, for he was also tainted by sin. All humanity has sinned and fallen short of God's glory (Romans 3:23), and as a result, the fullness of God's glory, which ought to be our source of life, became a threat of death to us.

But even so, God provided the means of maintaining a relationship with His people and sharing His life-giving presence. He instructed the Israelites to build a dwelling place for Him and instituted the sacrificial system to allow for His presence to remain with them. But even that was always intended to be temporary because God knew the people's hearts were too hard.

3 Read Exodus 40:34–38 again, and list out any descriptions you see of how God interacted with His people through the tabernacle. Do you see any connections between these details and the role that Jesus Christ would later come to fulfill?

The connection between the tabernacle and Jesus is made explicit in John 1:14. The Greek word in our English Bibles that is often translated as "dwelt" in this verse literally means to set up a tent (or tabernacle). John wants his readers to see that Exodus was just a foreshadowing of what was to come.

God met the Israelites in their wilderness wanderings. They were dwelling in tents; therefore, He came to dwell in a tent. He did this all in order to have a relationship with them—so that they would be His people and He would be their God. In the same way, God came for all humanity as we wandered through this broken world. We all are dwelling in mortal human flesh; therefore, our God took on that same human flesh.

He did all of this so that we can be His people—His children—and He can be our God. Because of His death and resurrection, humanity can be in the presence of God through His Holy Spirit, which dwells in each of us who believe.

4 Read Revelation 21:1–4. What do these verses reveal to us about God's ultimate plan and purpose for us and His creation?

Just like the Israelites awaited God's presence to at last bring them into the Promised Land, we also await the day when we will be brought to our final destination—when Jesus returns and restores all things. On that day, we will experience God's presence and glory to the fullest, and for eternity, we will say, "God's dwelling is with humanity" (Revelation 21:3).

Live it Out

1 Read Exodus 40:34–38 and John 1:10–14.

In this week's verses, we have seen how God—through His plan of redemption—has made it possible for His great glory to dwell with lowly, sinful, mortal human beings. First, He came to humanity in the tabernacle. Then He came in the person of Jesus Christ, God in human flesh. And finally, He will return in the last days and fully establish His presence in all the earth.

In the meantime, however, God has not left His people! The sacrifice of Christ made it possible for us to have access to His presence—to all of His glory and love. Jesus told His disciples that it was good for Him to return to heaven because then they would receive the Holy Spirit (John 16:7). The Bible teaches us that we now are the dwelling place of God, for the Holy Spirit—the Spirit of Christ—dwells in us (Colossians 1:27, Romans 8:10, 1 Corinthians 3:16).

REFLECT ON THIS WEEK'S VERSES AS YOU ANSWER THE FOLLOWING QUESTIONS:

2 In what ways do you see God's presence at work in your own life?

3 Do you truly believe you have access to the same God whose glory filled the tabernacle? Is that belief reflected in your prayers?

4 First Corinthians 6:19 tells us that we — the Church — are the body of Christ and, therefore, the dwelling place of God's Spirit. How should that truth influence the way you live?

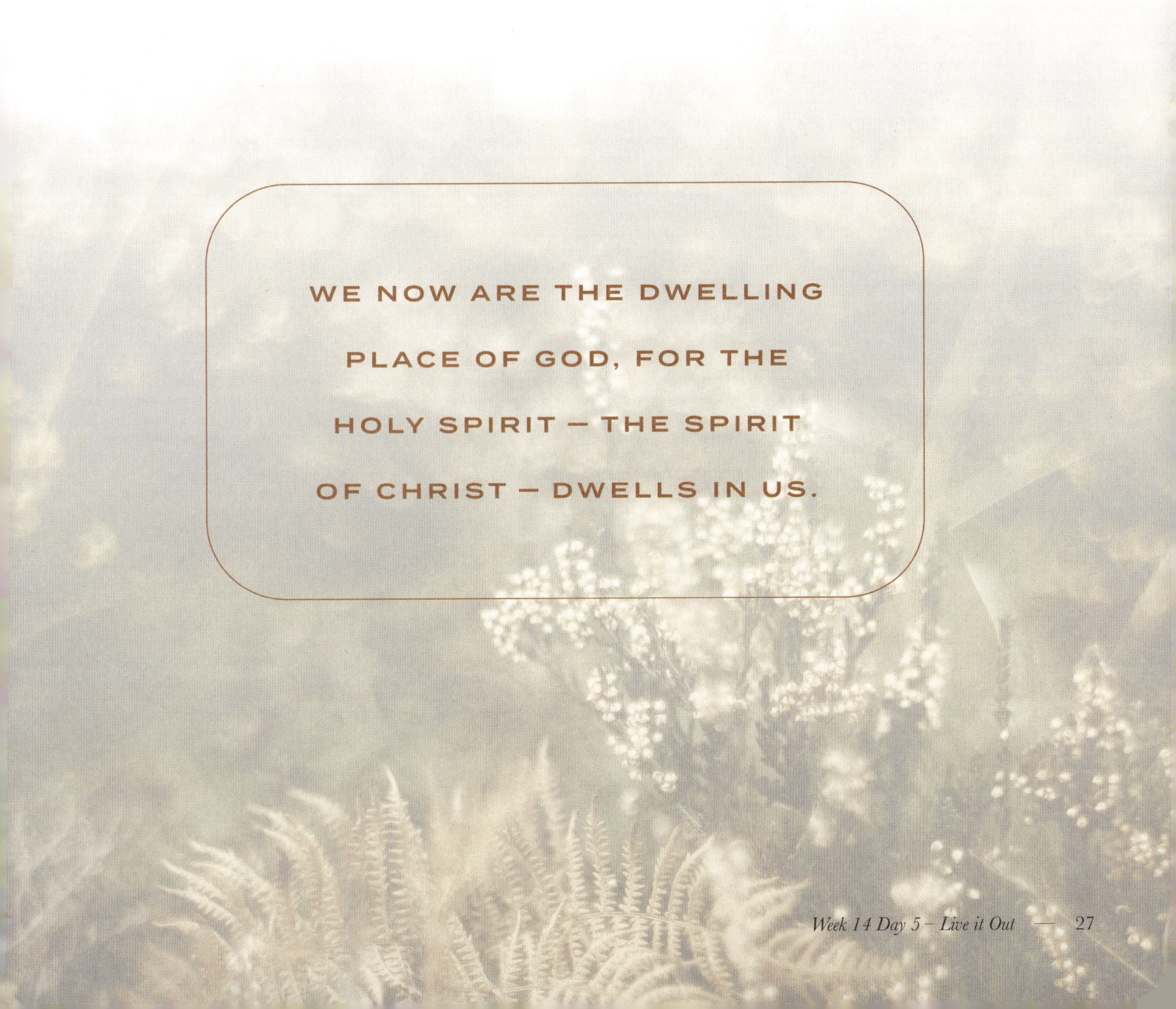

WE NOW ARE THE DWELLING PLACE OF GOD, FOR THE HOLY SPIRIT – THE SPIRIT OF CHRIST – DWELLS IN US.

Eden and the Tabernacle

The Bible contains numerous verbal and visual parallels between the tabernacle and the garden of Eden, indicating that we are meant to see Eden as a temple, a place where God Himself dwells. For example:

1A

GENESIS 3:8

God walked among the garden.

→

1B

LEVITICUS 26:12, DEUTERONOMY 23:14

God walked among the Israelites.

2A

GENESIS 3:24

Cherubim stood outside the garden, guarding the way to the Tree of Life.

→

2B

EXODUS 25:17–22; 26:1, 31

Statues of cherubim stood watch over the ark of the covenant, and curtains leading to the Most Holy Place had cherubim woven into them.

3A

GENESIS 2:15

Humanity was to "work" and "watch over" the garden.

→

3B

NUMBERS 3:7–8, 8:25–26, 18:5–6; 1 CHRONICLES 23:32; EZEKIEL 44:14

The priest's role in the tabernacle is described with these same Hebrew words.

4A

GENESIS 2:9

In the center of the garden stood the Tree of Life.

→

4B

EXODUS 25:31–40

The lampstand in the tabernacle was shaped like a tree, likely symbolizing the Tree of Life.

5A

GENESIS 3:24

The garden was entered from the east.

→

5B

NUMBERS 3:38

The tabernacle was entered from the east.

Introduction

WEEK FIFTEEN

This week, we will study the Day of Atonement detailed in Leviticus 16, alongside the complete, atoning work of Christ described in Hebrews 9:24–26. As you study, you will learn that the Old Testament's sacrificial system always pointed toward Jesus, for He single-handedly atoned for sin by sacrificing His life. Our sin was costly, but through Christ's work on the cross, we have gained freedom.

MARK IT UP

Old Testament Passage

Today, we will begin studying Leviticus 16, which outlines the Israelites' Day of Atonement—the day in which the priests completed sacrificial rituals to atone for the sins of God's people. By studying the Day of Atonement, we will better understand the weight of our sin and better marvel at Jesus's payment for our sin on the cross. Read Leviticus 16:20–22 multiple times and annotate, or mark up, the text as you read. For tips and examples on annotating, see page 196–207.

1. Highlight any words or phrases that point to Christ.

2. Make note of any attributes of God seen in the text.

3. Circle the verbs (or action words) present in this passage. What do these verbs teach you about this atonement ritual?

4. Draw a box around any unfamiliar words. Use a Bible dictionary or an online search engine to determine the meanings of these words. What did you learn?

5. Underline the first half of Leviticus 16:22. Why might God instruct the Israelites to send this goat into a "desolate land"?

LEVITICUS 16:20–22

20 "When he has finished making atonement for the most holy
place, the tent of meeting, and the altar, he is to present the
live male goat. 21 Aaron will lay both his hands on the head of
the live goat and confess over it all the Israelites' iniquities
and rebellious acts — all their sins. He is to put them on the
goat's head and send it away into the wilderness by the man
appointed for the task. 22 The goat will carry all their iniquities
into a desolate land, and the man will release it there."

atonement: God's forgiveness of sin and restoration of relationship with His people, typically by sacrifice. Ultimately, Jesus Christ is the atoning sacrifice for our sin.

Go Deeper

1 Read Leviticus 16:20–22.

The story of the Bible can be understood quite simply: God desires to dwell with His people. And yet, in Psalm 5:4, David teaches us that God does not delight in wickedness, and evil cannot dwell with Him. So how, then, can a holy God dwell with sinful people? Our good God made a way.

In Leviticus 16, God institutes an annual Day of Atonement in which the appointed high priest completes rituals so that God's people may be temporarily forgiven. With the completion of these rituals, God's presence can remain among His people. And therefore, their relationship with Him can be temporarily restored, for full and final restoration will come later through Christ.

The Day of Atonement is somber—a day set aside for Israel to humble themselves, to fast, and to acknowledge their sin before their holy God. Every detail of the ritual holds sacred significance. The goat described in Leviticus 16:22 is called a "scapegoat" by many translations. As the high priest confesses sins over this live goat, this goat bears the blame for the sins of God's people and is sent away into a desolate land. But the scapegoat is not the only goat involved in the Day of Atonement.

2 Read Leviticus 16:7–10 and Leviticus 16:20–22. What was the other goat's role in the Day of Atonement? What does this teach you about sin?

Sin has a cost: this cost is death. Yet, in God's kindness, He institutes a sacrificial system in which sins are pardoned by the death of an animal rather than the death of His people. By the blood of the first goat, the cost of the Israelites' sin is temporarily paid. But why does God demand blood as a payment for sins?

If we flip our Bibles all the way back to Genesis 2:17, God warns Adam of the consequence of eating from the Tree of the Knowledge of Good and Evil: death. Similarly, Leviticus 17:11 teaches us that blood is the representation of life, and therefore, the sacrifice of the goat fulfills the cost of sin communicated by God since the beginning of mankind. Animal sacrifices remind the Israelites of the weight of their sin.

And yet, the Day of Atonement includes two goats. One goat dies as a sin offering, and the other bears the sins of the people and carries them far from camp. Both goats communicate different attributes of God's character—His holiness and His mercy.

3 Read Leviticus 16:29–34. How often do the Israelites have to observe the Day of Atonement? What does this teach us about the goat's ability to atone for Israel's sin?

God instructs the Israelites to observe the Day of Atonement each year. However, the blood of the goat satisfies God's wrath against sin only temporarily. And so, on the tenth day of the seventh month of each year, the high priest again takes part in the bloody, costly ceremony of the Day of Atonement. This happens in order that God's people can be cleansed of sin and enjoy the presence of their Father—perhaps longing for a day when sacrifices are no longer necessary—when the cost of sin is paid forevermore.

4 Take a moment to pause and thank God for both His holiness and His mercy—so clearly displayed in Leviticus 16.

MARK IT UP

New Testament Passage

Now that we have studied how God made a way for the Israelites' sin to be forgiven through the annual Day of Atonement, we will turn our attention to the New Testament to see how Jesus forgives our sin once and for all. Read Hebrews 9:24–26 multiple times and annotate, or mark up, the text as you read. For tips and examples on annotating, see page 196–207.

1. Highlight any words or phrases that point to Christ.

2. Make note of any attributes of God seen in the text.

3. Highlight or underline any words or phrases that compare and contrast Jesus's sacrifice with the sacrifices of the Old Testament.

4. Now, draw a box around any conjunctions (i.e., words such as *for*, *and*, *nor*, *but*, *or*, *yet*, *so*). What do these words show you?

5. Circle any words that describe the frequency of sacrifices offered to God.

6. Once you have finished annotating the passage, consider why you think the author of Hebrews took such great care to distinguish between the high priests' sacrifices in the Old Testament and Jesus's sacrifice in the New. Jot your thoughts below.

HEBREWS 9:24–26

24 For Christ did not enter a sanctuary made with hands
(only a model of the true one) but into heaven itself, so that he
might now appear in the presence of God for us. 25 He did not
do this to offer himself many times, as the high priest enters
the sanctuary yearly with the blood of another. 26 Otherwise,
he would have had to suffer many times since the foundation
of the world. But now he has appeared one time, at the end
of the ages, for the removal of sin by the sacrifice of himself.

Make the Christ Connection

1 Read Leviticus 16:20–22 and Hebrews 9:24–26.

In Leviticus 16, we learn that Israel's Day of Atonement involved two goats—one that died as a sin offering and another that bore the sins of the Israelites and carried them far from camp. This sacred day on the Jewish calendar was solemn, tedious, and bloody and was not shrouded in celebration but in self-denial. The Israelites fasted, cleansed the temple from impurities, and acknowledged their sin before their holy God.

2 Read Leviticus 16:15–19. Where does the high priest bring the blood of the sacrificed goat? What does he do with it?

The blood of the sacrificed goat was to be brought into the innermost sanctuary of the tabernacle, where the presence of God dwelled. There, in the Most Holy Place in the Israelite camp, the high priest would sprinkle the blood of the goat upon the mercy seat to make atonement for the Israelites' impurities and rebellious acts (Leviticus 16:16–17).

3 Now, read Hebrews 9:24–26. What is similar about the high priest's sacrifice and Jesus's sacrifice? What is different?

The author of Hebrews makes a clear distinction between the high priests' sacrifices and the sacrifice of Jesus. Christ did not enter a sanctuary made by human hands, but rather, He entered heaven itself. Jesus did not present the blood of an animal before God; He presented His own blood—blood that is perfectly pure as a result of His sinless and unblemished life.

The author of Hebrews draws another distinction between the sacrifices of high priests and Jesus. Year after year, Israel gathered to observe the Day of Atonement. Goat after goat, ram after ram, no sacrifice was enough to cleanse God's people of their sin once and for all—until Jesus. Only Jesus's sacrifice is sufficient for the forgiveness of sin. God provided the perfect sacrifice, His only Son, to satisfy His own wrath against sin once and for all. Jesus is enough.

Jesus is the perfect sacrifice, the ultimate fulfillment of the goat's sacrifice on the Day of Atonement. But Jesus is not only the perfect sacrifice; Jesus is our perfect scapegoat. In Leviticus 16:20–22, we read that the scapegoat carried the sins of God's people to a desolate land, symbolizing God's forgiveness of sin.

4 Read 2 Corinthians 5:21. What does this verse say that Jesus became for us? How does this relate to the scapegoat?

As the high priest confessed the sins of Israel over the scapegoat, the scapegoat symbolically became sin. Similarly, 2 Corinthians 5:21 tells us that Jesus, the One who did not know sin, became sin for us so that in Him, we might become the righteousness of God. In Christ, the scapegoat and perfect sacrifice, our transgressions are carried as far as the east is from the west (Psalm 103:12). We receive full and final atonement, and we are clothed with His righteousness. His perfection is credited to our account.

Ultimately, the Day of Atonement points us toward our need for a permanent atonement of sin—an atonement achieved in Christ Jesus. Jesus's sacrifice is enough to cover all the sins of all God's people. Therefore, the yearly Day of Atonement is fulfilled by Jesus's all-encompassing sacrifice.

Live it Out

1 Read Leviticus 16:20–22 and Hebrews 9:24–26.

In today's modern context, church worship services do not include a ritual sacrifice. No blood is sprinkled upon a holy altar. No goat is sent into the wilderness. In fact, we would likely feel horrified by such events. On this side of the cross, we have no need to participate in an annual Day of Atonement. Our sins have been paid for in full by Christ's sacrifice. Calvary was the ultimate altar, and Good Friday was the ultimate Day of Atonement. Because Christ's blood is sufficient to cover the cost of our sin, we are freed from the rituals outlined in Leviticus 16.

However, just because we do not participate in an annual Day of Atonement does not mean we are exempt from mourning our sin and remembering its cost. On the contrary, even more so today, we behold Jesus's sacrifice and understand just how much our sin grieves God's heart. But God's hatred of sin motivated Him to move in love, to send His only Son to free His people from sin. God's hatred toward sin moves us to hate our own sin. God's extravagant love moves us to love.

This deeper understanding of the cost of sin moves us to obedience, for the atoning blood of Jesus is personal. God sees every sin—intentional and unintentional—you have ever committed, and He forgives each one fully through Jesus Christ. You can let go of the guilt you harbor in your heart and obey God in reverence of Christ's sacrifice, worshiping more deeply than ever before, for Jesus's blood was spilled so that you may have life and life abundant (John 10:10).

REFLECT ON THIS WEEK'S VERSES AS YOU ANSWER THE FOLLOWING QUESTIONS.

2 What does God's willingness to sacrifice His only Son to rid the world of sin communicate about the severity of sin?

3 How would your life look different if you truly hated your sin?

4 Write a prayer of thanksgiving for the atonement from sin that God provided through His Son, Jesus.

GOD'S EXTRAVAGANT LOVE MOVES US TO LOVE.

Introduction

WEEK SIXTEEN

This week, we will look at the account of the bronze snake in Numbers 21:4–9 and see how Jesus, in John 3:14–16, uses this incident in Israel's history to describe His own work. In comparing these passages, you will be encouraged to base your acceptance with God on what Jesus has done for you, not on what you have done for God.

MARK IT UP

Old Testament Passage

Today, we will study Numbers 21:4–9 and see how God's means of healing the Israelites points forward to what Jesus will accomplish on the cross. Read the passage multiple times and annotate, or mark up, the text as you read. For tips and examples on annotating, see page 196–207.

1. Highlight any words or phrases that point to Christ.

2. Make note of any attributes of God seen in the text.

3. Circle each thing that Israel complains about in this passage.

4. Underline God's response to the Israelites's sin and also His response to Moses's prayer.

5. How is God's wrath seen in this passage? How is God's mercy seen in it?

NUMBERS 21:4–9

4 Then they set out from Mount Hor by way of the Red Sea to
bypass the land of Edom, but the people became impatient because
of the journey. 5 The people spoke against God and Moses: “Why
have you led us up from Egypt to die in the wilderness? There is
no bread or water, and we detest this wretched food!” 6 Then the
Lord sent poisonous snakes among the people, and they bit them
so that many Israelites died. 7 The people then came to Moses and
said, “We have sinned by speaking against the Lord and against
you. Intercede with the Lord so that he will take the snakes away
from us.” And Moses interceded for the people. 8 Then the Lord
said to Moses, “Make a snake image and mount it on a pole. When
anyone who is bitten looks at it, he will recover.” 9 So Moses made
a bronze snake and mounted it on a pole. Whenever someone
was bitten, and he looked at the bronze snake, he recovered.

Go Deeper

1 Read Numbers 21:4–9.

The book of Numbers covers a lot of ground and serves as a transition point in the biblical story. In the book of Exodus, God rescued the Israelites from slavery in Egypt so that He could bring them to the land of Canaan that He had promised to give them (Exodus 6:2–8). But first, He brought Israel to Mount Sinai, where He gave them His law and entered into a covenant relationship with them. From Exodus 19 through the book of Leviticus, Israel is encamped at Sinai. But in Numbers, God at last leads His people to the brink of the Promised Land. As they near Canaan, Moses sends out twelve spies to investigate the land and its current inhabitants—whom they will have to battle.

2 Numbers 13:25–14:9. What report do the spies bring back about the land and its people? How do the Israelites respond to this report (Numbers 14:1–4)? What do Joshua and Caleb tell the people (Numbers 14:5–9)?

God has already demonstrated His power and willingness to help the Israelites by bringing them up out of slavery in Egypt. And He has promised to give them the land of Canaan. But at the report of the spies, the people do not trust God to come through for them again. In response, God tells the Israelites that they will wander in the wilderness one year for every day the spies were exploring Canaan—forty years in all. The generation that had been brought out of Egypt will pass away in the wilderness and not enter the land (Numbers 14:26–35).

By Numbers 21, the older generation has passed away, along with Moses's brother, Aaron (Numbers 20:22–29). The forty years are nearing their end, and the next generation will soon enter Canaan.

3 In the chart below, write down what you see both the old and new generations doing in the listed passages. What similarities do you notice between them? What conclusions can we draw about this new generation?

Old Generation	New Generation
Exodus 17:1–3	Numbers 20:1–5
Numbers 11:4–6, 14:2–3	Numbers 21:4–5

It is clear from Numbers 20 and 21 that the new generation is not so different from the old, being just as prone to grumble against God when hardships arise. Therefore, Numbers 21:4–9 is a vivid reminder that sin deserves God's judgment and that "the wages of sin is death" (Romans 6:23).

But it is also a reminder of God's mercy. Realizing their foolishness, the Israelites confess their sin, and God instructs Moses to put a bronze snake up on a pole. Though the Israelites deserve to die for their sin, God promises that anyone who looks upon the lifted snake will live.

4 Spend time meditating on God's mercy and write out a prayer, thanking Him for how He has shown mercy to you.

MARK IT UP

New Testament Passage

Today, we will turn to the Gospel of John, where Jesus discusses the bronze snake incident from Numbers 24:4–9 with a prominent religious leader named Nicodemus. Read John 3:14–16 multiple times and annotate, or mark up, the text as you read. For tips and examples on annotating, see page 196–207.

1. Highlight any words or phrases that point to Christ.
2. Make note of any attributes of God seen in the text.
3. Circle any language from Numbers 21:4–9 that you see reflected in these verses.
4. Underline the references to death and life.

JOHN 3:14–16

14 "Just as Moses lifted up the snake in the wilderness, so the
Son of Man must be lifted up, 15 so that everyone who believes
in him may have eternal life. 16 For God loved the world in
this way: He gave his one and only Son, so that everyone
who believes in him will not perish but have eternal life."

Make the Christ Connection

1 Read Numbers 21:4–9 and John 3:1–21.

A Pharisee named Nicodemus—who respects Jesus but does not quite grasp who He is or what He has come to do—approaches Jesus. And in the course of their conversation, Jesus clues Nicodemus in, telling him that being born again is a prerequisite for entrance into God's kingdom. Thinking Jesus is referring to being physically born again, Nicodemus is understandably confused. But Jesus clarifies that He is referring to being "born of water and the Spirit" (John 3:5). He also mentions that Nicodemus, as a teacher of Israel, should not be surprised by what Jesus is saying (John 3:7, 11). In other words, the Old Testament—which Nicodemus has spent His life studying—speaks to the need for being "born of water and the Spirit" (John 3:5).

But where does the Old Testament say this? Most likely, Jesus is articulating what God spoke through the prophet Ezekiel centuries earlier.

2 Read Ezekiel 36:25–27. What parallels do you see between this passage and what Jesus says in John 3:5?

As we saw on Day 2 of this week, rebelling against God was nothing new for the nation of Israel. So persistent was Israel's sin over the centuries that God eventually removed them from Canaan, or the Promised Land, and sent them into exile. But it was in their exile that God promised, through the prophet Ezekiel, to cleanse His people with water and give them a new spirit. They would be forgiven and enabled to start living in obedience to God. And this, according to Jesus, is what it means to be born again.

As Jesus speaks with Nicodemus, He appeals to the account of the bronze snake from Numbers 21:4–9 (John 3:14–15). Jesus has been speaking to Nicodemus about the need for God to provide new life, and here, He makes the point that just as God gave life to Israel in the wilderness, so He is granting the new life required to enter the kingdom of God. And God will once again grant this new life through a *lifting up*—not of a bronze snake but of Jesus, His "one and only Son" (John 3:16).

3 John 3:16 may be the most famous verse in all of the Bible. How does the connection Jesus makes between Himself and the bronze snake help us appreciate what this verse says?

The language of Jesus being "lifted up" shows up a few times in John's Gospel (John 3:14; 8:28; 12:32, 34), and it carries two meanings. First, the lifting up refers to His crucifixion. Just as the snake was lifted up on a pole, so too will Jesus be lifted up on a cross. But the lifting up also refers to Jesus's exaltation. Because of His death, resurrection, and ascension to heaven, all who look to Jesus in faith "will not perish but have eternal life" (John 3:16).

4 Spend time praising God for the eternal life He has given to you through the lifting up of Jesus.

Pharisee: A Jewish religious leader known for strict observance of the Law.

Live it Out

1 Read Numbers 21:4–9 and John 3:14–16.

There are many things we can learn from the bronze snake incident in Numbers 21:4–9. First, we learn of the fallen condition of humanity. This "new" generation of Israelites is much the same as the old. They instinctively turn against God and doubt His goodness. Second, we learn that God is holy and just, and He will punish sin. But third, we learn that God is merciful and responds favorably when people confess their sins.

If this passage demonstrates that "the wages of sin is death," it also demonstrates that "the gift of God is eternal life in Christ Jesus our Lord" (Romans 6:23). Jesus is God's servant whom Isaiah said would "be raised and lifted up and greatly exalted" (Isaiah 52:13). Because of His death on the cross, we receive what we do not deserve: everlasting life.

REFLECT ON THIS WEEK'S VERSES AS YOU ANSWER THE FOLLOWING QUESTIONS.

2 The Israelites had a habit of complaining about God when life became hard. In what ways can you relate? When do you tend to grumble and think that God does not know what is best for you?

3. Jesus speaks of new life in John 3. How have you seen God at work in your life? Which of your behaviors have been impacted?

4. How can these passages encourage you to be honest about your sin? When you feel guilt and shame over the sins you have committed, what encouragement can you take from the verses we have looked at this week?

GOD IS MERCIFUL AND RESPONDS FAVORABLY WHEN PEOPLE CONFESS THEIR SINS.

Introduction

WEEK SEVENTEEN

This week, we will trace the theme of the Shema—the basic confession of faith in Judaism that God is One, and He alone should be worshiped—through Deuteronomy 6:4–5 and Matthew 22:37–40. In doing so, you will be reminded that Jesus worships God perfectly and enables believers to give God the worship He deserves. These reminders will encourage you to put God first in your life as you love Him and others in response to the gospel.

MARK IT UP

Old Testament Passage

Today, we will begin the week by studying Deuteronomy 6:4–5. As we do, we will learn of God's command to love Him with all of who we are. Read this passage two or three times and annotate, or mark up, the text as you read. For tips and examples on annotating, see page 196–207.

1. Highlight any words or phrases that point to Christ.

2. Make note of any attributes of God seen in the text.

3. Circle the word "one" in verse 4.

4. Underline every mention of the word "all."

5. What is the command in verse 5?

DEUTERONOMY 6:4–5

4 “Listen, Israel: The LORD our God, the LORD is
one. 5 Love the LORD your God with all your heart,
with all your soul, and with all your strength.”

Go Deeper

1 Read Deuteronomy 6:4–5.

Each one of us is made to worship. And although our hearts are pulled in different directions toward various objects of worship, our hearts are designed to love one thing—or rather, one *Person*—above all: the Lord. In Deuteronomy 6:4–5, God gives the Israelites an important command, reminding them of what the object of their devotion should be—Himself.

The book of Deuteronomy takes place toward the end of Moses's life, as a new generation of Israelites are poised to enter the Promised Land. With this in mind, Moses leaves the people with some final reminders, including repeating the Ten Commandments (originally given to their parents and grandparents in Exodus 20) to this new generation. The first two commandments demand worship to God alone, as God commands the Israelites to have no other gods apart from Him and to make no idols for themselves (Deuteronomy 5:6–10). Today's passage connects to these commands, as they instruct total devotion to the Lord.

This is important for the Israelites because they have been called to be God's chosen people. God brought the Israelites out of slavery in order to form them into a nation for His own glory. This command is also important because the Israelites have left Egypt, a nation of people who worship false gods, and now they are heading to Canaan, a land filled with people who also worship false Gods. In order for Israel to reflect God's glory to the nations, they need to obey the Lord wholeheartedly.

2 How would Israel worshiping God wholeheartedly be different from how the other nations worship? Consider Psalm 96.

Israel can obey the Lord wholeheartedly by loving Him with all their heart, soul, and strength—in other words, with all of themselves. There is to be no part of the Israelites that does not give God the worship He so deserves. To be wholehearted in their worship, the Israelites must turn away from any other objects of worship. They must forsake the gods that the nations around them worship to worship the one true God. This is why God declares, "the LORD is one" in verse 4. God is the one true God who rules and reigns over all of creation. Unlike the other nations, the Israelites are to view God as the only God who is sovereign over all and worship Him alone.

3 What would it look like practically for God to be the sole object of Israel's worship? What does this mean for our own lives?

Deuteronomy 6:4 begins what would come to be known as the Shema. These words would become a prayer that the Israelites would pray to remind themselves of the exclusivity of their worship. Over time, this prayer would become an important part of Jewish history, and ancient Jews would pray these words every morning and evening.

As the second-generation Israelites prepare to enter the Promised Land, Moses reminds them that they must make the command found in Deuteronomy 6:4–5 a priority—because their ancestors have already failed to do so. The first generation chose not to listen to the Lord, and in doing so, they were kept from entering the Promised Land. Now, this second generation has the chance to respond differently than their ancestors by giving God the worship He deserves.

4 Ask the Lord to help you worship Him wholeheartedly in response to who He is, what He has done, and what He will do.

MARK IT UP

New Testament Passage

Now that we have studied the Shema, we will turn to the New Testament to see how Jesus repeats and fulfills these words during His ministry. Read Matthew 22:37–40 two or three times and annotate, or mark up, the text as you read. For tips and examples on annotating, see page 196–207.

1. Highlight any words or phrases that point to Christ.

2. Make note of any attributes of God seen in the text.

3. Underline what the greatest command is.

4. Circle the second command.

5. According to verse 40, what depends on these two commands? What do you think this means?

6. How are these two commands related?

MATTHEW 22:37–40

37 He said to him, "Love the Lord your God with all your
heart, with all your soul, and with all your mind. 38 This is
the greatest and most important command. 39 The second
is like it: Love your neighbor as yourself. 40 All the Law
and the Prophets depend on these two commands."

Make the Christ Connection

1 Read Deuteronomy 6:4–5 and Matthew 22:37–40.

The second generation of Israelites had the chance to be different from their ancestors by giving God their complete worship. But sadly, they failed. They turned away from the Lord and became like the nations around them by worshiping false gods (Judges 2:11–13). The Israelites' failure in this way points to the failure of each one of us who falls short of giving God true and total worship. But there is One person who has never failed in worship and obedience to God: Jesus Christ. Through Him, we can be forgiven of our wayward worship and empowered to worship the Lord above all else.

In Matthew 22:37–40, Jesus responds to a question asked by an expert in the Law in verse 36: "Teacher, which command in the law is the greatest?" The expert in the Law asks this question to test Jesus's view of the Law. If Jesus sees one particular law as carrying more weight than the others, the Pharisees can falsely accuse Jesus of not viewing the other laws as important, hurting Jesus's reputation. While Jesus does respond by choosing one commandment over the others, His answer declares the importance of obeying all of God's law. His answer shows how love for God will result in obedience. Therefore, the rest of God's commands will be obeyed as His people put Him first and worship Him alone.

Jesus could have simply stopped with that first commandment in Matthew 22:37, but Jesus goes on to give a second command in connection to the first. This second command comes from Leviticus 19:18, which reads, "Do not take revenge or bear a grudge against members of your community, but love your neighbor as yourself; I am the LORD." In giving this command, Jesus teaches that love for God results in love for others. Those who love the Lord will respond by loving those around them. When we love God and others, we fulfill the purpose of the Law (Matthew 22:40, Galatians 5:13–14).

2 Read Romans 13:8–10. What does this passage say about love and its relationship with the Law?

However, no person loves God perfectly or always loves their neighbor as themself. Therefore, we all fall short of these two commandments. Only Jesus loves God with all of His being and loves His neighbor as Himself perfectly. Even when Satan tempts Jesus in the wilderness, Jesus responds by saying, "For it is written: Worship the Lord your God, and serve only him" (Matthew 4:10). Jesus obeyed the Lord perfectly, to the extent that He willingly laid down His life for us on the cross.

3 Why do we fail to worship God as we should? Consider Romans 1:18–25.

It is through Christ's death and resurrection that we are able to reflect Christ's obedience and worship. Jesus forgives us when we fail to worship the Lord with all of our hearts, and it is because of His salvation and the power of the Spirit that we are able to rightly worship Him alone. And even when we do fail, we are covered by God's grace. Such grace motivates us to worship the Lord joyfully and obey Him in all that we say and do.

4 Thank the Lord for giving you forgiveness through Christ for any wayward worship. Ask Him to help you respond to the gospel with joyful obedience to Him.

Live it Out

1 Read Deuteronomy 6:4–5 and Matthew 22:37–40.

In response to God's grace and Christ's salvation, we worship the Lord joyfully. We look to God alone for our source of satisfaction and seek to obey Him in all that we say and do. And as we worship the Lord and love Him above all else (Matthew 22:37), we are compelled to love others (1 John 4:7, 11). Our love for God flows outward from our hearts to those around us.

However, loving God wholeheartedly and loving our neighbors as ourselves are hard commands to obey because of our sinful flesh. Yet, when we meditate on the gospel, we are reminded that Christ enables and empowers us to love both God and others. We are also reminded of God's great love for us through Christ (1 John 4:9–10). Therefore, if we find that our love for the Lord has grown cold, we can allow the truth of the gospel to warm our hearts.

The command to love God with all of who we are should also challenge us to look at our lives and see if there is anything we are worshiping other than the Lord (Deuteronomy 6:4–5). We should ask ourselves: *What is taking first place in my heart? What am I looking to and depending on besides God?* And with the help of the Holy Spirit, we can turn from these things to worship the Lord alone.

REFLECT ON THIS WEEK'S VERSES AS YOU ANSWER THE FOLLOWING QUESTIONS.

2 What keeps you from worshiping God wholeheartedly?

3 How does the Holy Spirit help you worship the Lord wholeheartedly?

4 What changes do you need to make, with the help of the Spirit, to put God first?

CHRIST ENABLES AND EMPOWERS US TO LOVE BOTH GOD AND OTHERS.

Introduction

WEEK EIGHTEEN

This week, we will trace the themes of blessings and curses through Deuteronomy 11:26–32 and Galatians 3:10–14. In doing so, we will see how Jesus became cursed and bore the penalty of our sin so that we might be blessed. In response, you will be encouraged to rejoice in Christ's sacrifice and challenged to trust in God's Spirit to make us holy.

MARK IT UP

Old Testament Passage

Today, we will begin studying Deuteronomy 11:26–32 and start to see Christ through the theme of blessings and curses in Scripture. Read the passage multiple times and annotate, or mark up, the text as you read. For tips and examples on annotating, see page 196–207.

1. Highlight any words or phrases that point to Christ.

2. Make note of any attributes of God seen in the text.

3. Circle each time the word "blessing" is used.

4. Underline each time the word "curse" is used.

5. Who is speaking in this passage, and to whom are they speaking?

DEUTERONOMY 11:26–32

26 "Look, today I set before you a blessing and a curse: 27 there will
be a blessing, if you obey the commands of the LORD your God I am
giving you today, 28 and a curse, if you do not obey the commands
of the LORD your God and you turn aside from the path I command
you today by following other gods you have not known. 29 When the
LORD your God brings you into the land you are entering to possess,
you are to proclaim the blessing at Mount Gerizim and the curse at
Mount Ebal. 30 Aren't these mountains across the Jordan, beyond the
western road in the land of the Canaanites, who live in the Arabah,
opposite Gilgal, near the oaks of Moreh? 31 For you are about to cross
the Jordan to enter and take possession of the land the LORD your
God is giving you. When you possess it and settle in it, 32 be careful
to follow all the statutes and ordinances I set before you today."

Go Deeper

1 Read Deuteronomy 11.

What is the most compelling monologue you have ever heard? It could be a university lecture or a sermon that captivates your attention. God's chosen people, the Israelites, are in the midst of hearing a compelling message of their own. The book of Deuteronomy is a series of speeches that Moses speaks to the people of Israel as God's prophet and messenger during their time in the wilderness after being delivered from slavery in Egypt. It is here in the wilderness that they learn more about the character of the God who delivered them.

2 Read Deuteronomy 10:21–22. What does the word "therefore" refer to in Deuteronomy 11:1? Why should the Israelites keep God's commands?

God promised to lead the Israelites into a land of their own, but as they wander in the wilderness, Moses must remind them of who they are and, more importantly, whose they are. Though God has delivered them from Pharaoh's oppressive rule, the Israelites still turn away to worship other gods while wandering in the wilderness (Deuteronomy 9:15–24). Moses cautions them again to pay close attention to God's statutes and speaks to the people about the outcome of following God's commands and the consequences of their disobedience. He reminds them that they are to teach these commands to their children so that future generations learn to fear the Lord and keep His statutes, as well.

3 What did God say would happen if the Israelites were obedient?

4 What did God say would happen if the Israelites were disobedient?

The result of obedience to God is blessing. If they are obedient, the people will enjoy the fruit of the land and the fruit of their labor (Deuteronomy 11:14). They will experience God's hand of provision and have peace with the surrounding nations. They will also be a blessing to those around them and have the assurance of God's presence and protection. However, if the Israelites do not keep God's commands, they will reap curses for themselves. In choosing to disobey, they will forfeit God's blessing and lose the guarantee of His protection.

5 How does forgetting God's past acts of faithfulness lead to sin?

6 Write a short prayer, asking God to help you to remember His kindness.

MARK IT UP

New Testament Passage

Over the past two days, we have seen the promise of blessings or curses that Moses laid out for the Israelites before they entered the Promised Land. Today, we will turn to the New Testament to see how Jesus came and took on the curse for us so that we might be blessed. Read Galatians 3:10–14 multiple times and annotate, or mark up, the text as you read. For tips and examples on annotating, see page 196–207.

1. Highlight any words or phrases that point to Christ.

2. Make note of any attributes of God seen in the text.

3. Circle each instance where the word "curse" is used.

4. Underline each instance where the word "law" is used.

5. Highlight each instance where the word "faith" is used.

6. Who is speaking in this passage, and who are they speaking to?

7. Why is the author writing to this group of people? (Hint: you may need to consult a study Bible or an outside resource, such as *The Bible Handbook* from The Daily Grace Co.®, to answer this question.)

GALATIANS 3:10–14

10 For all who rely on the works of the law are under a curse,
because it is written, Everyone who does not do everything written
in the book of the law is cursed.
11 Now it is clear that no one is
justified before God by the law, because the righteous will live
by faith.
12 But the law is not based on faith; instead, the one who
does these things will live by them.
13 Christ redeemed us from the
curse of the law by becoming a curse for us, because it is written,
Cursed is everyone who is hung on a tree.
14 The purpose was
that the blessing of Abraham would come to the Gentiles by Christ
Jesus, so that we could receive the promised Spirit through faith.

Make the Christ Connection

1 Read Deuteronomy 11:26–32 and Galatians 3:10–14.

As we know, it did not take long for God's people to disobey His commands. Once again, they failed to remember what He had done for them and their ancestors. Still, God would lead them into the Promised Land of Canaan, but their idolatrous hearts would keep them from obeying Him. Though God, through Moses, clearly told the Israelites of the blessings and curses and the choice set before them, they chose to disobey God rather than pursuing blessing.

As a result of their disobedience, Israel heaped curses upon themselves that led to their eventual exile and destruction. God had promised blessing to them if they were obedient but curses if they were not, and they had chosen the latter. They were clearly unable to obey God in their own power. Similarly, when we examine our own lives, we see that our fate is the same as that of Israel. We are unable to exhibit the holiness and purity that God requires, quick to forget who God is and what He has done. In our sin, we have wrought curses upon ourselves—the consequences of our sin—the worst of which is death and eternal separation from God.

2 Read Galatians 1:6–9. Why would following a false gospel lead to a curse?

The Israelites' inability to be obedient exposed their need for a Savior. In His mercy, God sent Jesus as this promised Savior to take on the penalty of sin for us. In His perfect obedience to God, Jesus secured God's blessing for us by living a perfect life. He removed the curse of sin from us by becoming cursed Himself. When Jesus hung on the cross, He incurred the curse of God. In His rising from the grave, Christ defeated death and now reigns victorious over sin and death. This is the gospel. Jesus removed the curse of the Law by fulfilling it and by receiving the consequence of sin—death—on our behalf. Now, by placing our faith in Him, we are no longer under a curse, but through Christ's righteousness, we are blessed.

3 We are no longer under the obligation of fulfilling the entire Law on our own. How do we now receive God's blessing?

In Galatians 3, Paul has grown frustrated with the Galatians; they have forgotten what Jesus has done for them. Just as the Israelites forgot God's great deeds on their behalf, so the Galatians now forget that blessing is found through faith in Christ alone. The churches of Galatia find themselves under the influence of men who try to convince them that they must earn God's blessing by their own merit. As Paul had told them before, this is impossible. The only way that anyone can be righteous is through faith in Jesus.

4 Write a prayer of gratitude, thanking Jesus for becoming a curse on our behalf so that we might live by faith.

Live it Out

1 Read Deuteronomy 11:26–32 and Galatians 3:10–14.

Picture yourself trying to lift heavy gym equipment. No matter how hard you try, you cannot move it. And not only this, but you are in danger of serious injury because the weight is threatening to crush you. Jesus is the One who lifts the heavy burden of sin's curse for us. We could never do it on our own, and God knew that. He could have left us to rightfully experience the full consequences of our sin—He would have been justified in doing so. Yet, in His infinite love, mercy, and compassion toward us, He sent Jesus. Christ became a curse for us and, in Him, we become righteous before God.

Because of Jesus, we are blessed with every spiritual blessing in the heavens (Ephesians 1:3). Because we are saved by faith and because we live by faith, we do not place our hope in following the rules, but we trust in God's Spirit to lead us into godliness. The gospel is good news: we are free from sin and death, free from the curse, and eternally blessed.

REFLECT ON THIS WEEK'S VERSES AS YOU ANSWER THE FOLLOWING QUESTIONS.

2 How should being free from the curse of sin affect your daily life?

3. Take a moment with the Lord in prayer, rejoicing that as a believer, you are no longer under a curse but eternally blessed in Christ.

4. Take some time to reflect on the blessings you have in Christ. Make a list of three or four of them.

THE GOSPEL IS GOOD NEWS: WE ARE FREE FROM SIN AND DEATH, FREE FROM THE CURSE, AND ETERNALLY BLESSED.

Blessings and Curses

As we studied Deuteronomy 11:26–32 this week, we saw the blessings and curses the Israelites could expect, depending on their actions, when they entered the Promised Land. Similarly, in Deuteronomy 28, Moses again lists out many of the blessings they will enjoy in the land if they are obedient to God's law. But he also warns them of the curses they will experience if they rebel against God. Below is a sampling of these blessings and curses.

BLESSINGS

If Israel is faithful to God in the land, they will be blessed with:

Numerous offspring

Abundant produce

Plentiful rain

Victory in battle

Full barns

Success in all their endeavors

Recognition from the nations that God is with them

CURSES

If Israel is unfaithful to God in the land, they will be cursed with:

Sickness and disease

Famine

Drought

Defeat in battle

Loss of possessions

Locusts that will eat their crops

Being plundered by other nations

Removal from the Promised Land

BECAUSE OF JESUS, WE ARE BLESSED WITH EVERY SPIRITUAL BLESSING IN THE HEAVENS (EPHESIANS 1:3).

Introduction

WEEK NINETEEN

This week, we will look at God's promise to speak to His people as we follow the themes of God's voice and the prophets through Deuteronomy 18:15–19 and Hebrews 1:1–2. Through these passages, we will learn that Jesus is the ultimate Prophet who speaks the words of God, and we will be encouraged to listen to God by studying Christ throughout Scripture.

MARK IT UP

Old Testament Passage

Today, we will begin studying Deuteronomy 18:15–19, and as we do so, we will see God's promise to send a prophet who will speak His Word. Read the passage multiple times and annotate, or mark up, the text as you read. For tips and examples on annotating, see page 196–207.

1. Highlight any words or phrases that point to Christ.

2. Make note of any attributes of God seen in the text.

3. Make note of verses 18–19. In a different color, highlight words in these verses that point toward the role of a prophet.

4. Circle any words, pronouns, or descriptions that point to God. What does He promise to do for Israel?

5. Underline references to the people of Israel.

DEUTERONOMY 18:15–19

15 “The LORD your God will raise up for you a prophet like me from
among your own brothers. You must listen to him. 16 This is what
you requested from the LORD your God at Horeb on the day of the
assembly when you said, “Let us not continue to hear the voice
of the LORD our God or see this great fire any longer, so that we
will not die!” 17 Then the LORD said to me, ‘They have spoken well.
18 I will raise up for them a prophet like you from among their
brothers. I will put my words in his mouth, and he will tell them
everything I command him. 19 I will hold accountable whoever
does not listen to my words that he speaks in my name.”

Go Deeper

1 Read Deuteronomy 18:15–19.

At this point in Israel's history, God is finally about to lead the Israelites into the Promised Land, and through Moses, He is in the process of repeating His Law to this new generation of Israelites. It is in the middle of this list of commands that Moses relays this promise from God: that He will raise up a prophet like Moses from the Israelite people.

2 This passage, specifically Deuteronomy 18:16, recounts a prior event in Israel's history. Read about this event in Exodus 20:18–21 and again in Deuteronomy 5:22–33. Why do the people need God to speak through Moses?

When the Israelites first arrived at Mount Sinai (Exodus 19), God's presence had come to rest on the top of the mountain, and it was intense. With His presence came darkness, fire, thunder, and lightning. The people could not go up the mountain or even touch it without the risk of death, but they gathered around its base and heard the audible voice of God give the Ten Commandments to Moses for the first time.

The people were terrified. They could not handle the presence and voice of God—even from a distance—and they begged Moses to relay God's words to them so that they would not have to hear from God directly. Deuteronomy 5:28–31 tells us that God commends the Israelites for this request and agrees to speak to them through Moses.

3 What does this interaction between God and the Israelites teach us about God?

It might be puzzling to us that God's own people are afraid of Him. Yet, for perspective, consider this: such an experience of hearing directly from God might be like standing at the bottom of an erupting volcano in the middle of a hurricane. Moses told them that God revealed Himself to them in this way so that they would fear Him and obey His commands (Exodus 20:20).

God was showing them the stark contrast between Himself and them—the contrast between Him and the people He created! He is the Creator of all things, a power we cannot even begin to comprehend. He is perfect goodness and eternal. What are we, in comparison? We are small, frail, sinful, and capable of death. We cannot compare to His power and glory, and that should make us fearful.

But these passages (Exodus 20:18–21, Deuteronomy 18:15–19) also show us God's compassion on the Israelites. He knew His holiness was too much for them in their sinful and mortal state. So, once they had seen Him and heard His great power—once they knew He was to be feared—He provided another way for them to continue to hear His voice and commands.

Moses, then, spoke the words of God to the people. He told them God's commandments and what was required of them to fulfill His covenant with them—that they would be His people and He would be their God. But now, in Deuteronomy, Moses is nearing the end of His life and cannot be with them as they enter the Promised Land. So, he assures the Israelites that God will not abandon them but will raise up another prophet like Moses himself to continue speaking the words of God to the people (Deuteronomy 18:15).

5 How do you think the Israelites felt, knowing that even though Moses would soon die, they would have another prophet to speak God's words to them?

MARK IT UP

New Testament Passage

Today, we will turn to the book of Hebrews to see how Jesus is the true and better Prophet that Moses pointed toward in Deuteronomy 18:15–19. Read Hebrews 1:1–2 multiple times and annotate, or mark up, the text as you read. For tips and examples on annotating, see page 196–207.

1 Highlight any words or phrases that point to Christ.

2 Make note of any attributes of God seen in the text.

3 Circle any words or pronouns that refer to Jesus.

4 Underline the references to time periods. To what points in time are these instances referring?

5 What do the prophets (mentioned in verse 1) speak about? Read Acts 3:22–26 to help you answer this question.

HEBREWS 1:1–2

1 Long ago God spoke to our ancestors by the prophets at
different times and in different ways. 2 In these last days,
he has spoken to us by his Son. God has appointed him
heir of all things and made the universe through him.

Make the Christ Connection

1 Read Deuteronomy 18:15–19 and Hebrews 1:1–2.

The prophets—from Moses onward—delivered the words and commands of God to the people. Deuteronomy 5:30–31 tells us that the goal of the prophetic office was that the people would know the commands of God and live under them when they made it to the Promised Land. But as the Old Testament continues, we see that even with all the prophets who came after Moses, the people could not keep God's commandments and consistently turned to other gods.

2 Read Acts 3:22–26. These verses speak to Jesus's role as a prophet. How does Jesus fulfill this prophetic office—or, in other words, how does Jesus fulfill the role of prophet?

Humanity needed a better prophet—one who could actually change the hearts of the people and bring them into the eternal Promised Land. Jesus is a better prophet, for unlike Moses and all the prophets after him, He does not merely relay the words of God—He is the Word of God, God Himself in the flesh (John 1:1, 14).

Peter says in Acts 3:22–26 that Jesus is the One spoken of in Deuteronomy 18 and that He was foretold by all the prophets of the Old Testament. Hebrews 1:1–2 tells us that God now speaks through His Son, Jesus, rather than any other prophets. He is the true Prophet—the Messiah—who will bring about the blessing God promised to Israel and to the entire world. Through His words, humanity can find eternal life.

3 Read Hebrews 2:14–15. How does this relate to what you read in Exodus 20 on Day 2 of this week's study?

Before Jesus came to earth, whenever God revealed Himself to people, they were afraid. They hid their faces from the glory of our Holy God, often falling down in worship. They knew they could not handle Him, His presence, and His voice directly, for they were sinners in the presence of a holy God.

But now, God's presence and God's Word bring life through the death and resurrection of Jesus. The same God behind the fire and the storm at Mount Sinai took on human flesh and walked among His people. Not only that, but He died so that His people could be set free from the power and fear of death. Those who look to and trust in Jesus as the true Prophet of God—the One through whom He speaks and shares His presence—will be able to walk with Him into eternal life.

4 Pray and thank God for sending Jesus, the true Prophet.

Live it Out

1 Read Deuteronomy 18:15–19 and Hebrews 1:1–2.

The Old Testament passages we have covered this week in Deuteronomy 18 and Exodus 20 show us that the presence and voice of God are not things we should take lightly. His power and glory exceed our comprehension. However, God has not merely demonstrated His power to us but also His compassion. We see such evidence of God's compassion on display through the gift of Jesus Christ—God's Word made flesh who came to dwell with us (John 1:14).

As Hebrews 1:1–2 taught us, Jesus is the true and better Prophet. But the author of Hebrews also goes on to tell us that Jesus is "the radiance of God's glory and the exact expression of His nature" (Hebrews 1:3). In other words, God has made a way for us to experience His presence and His voice through Jesus Christ. Indeed, through Jesus, God has brought us Himself.

REFLECT ON THIS TRUTH AS YOU ANSWER THESE QUESTIONS.

2 What does it mean for you to fear God?

3 How might you balance a fear of God with a knowledge of His compassion?

4. Read Hebrews 2:14–15 again. Do you truly believe that Christ has delivered you from the fear of death?

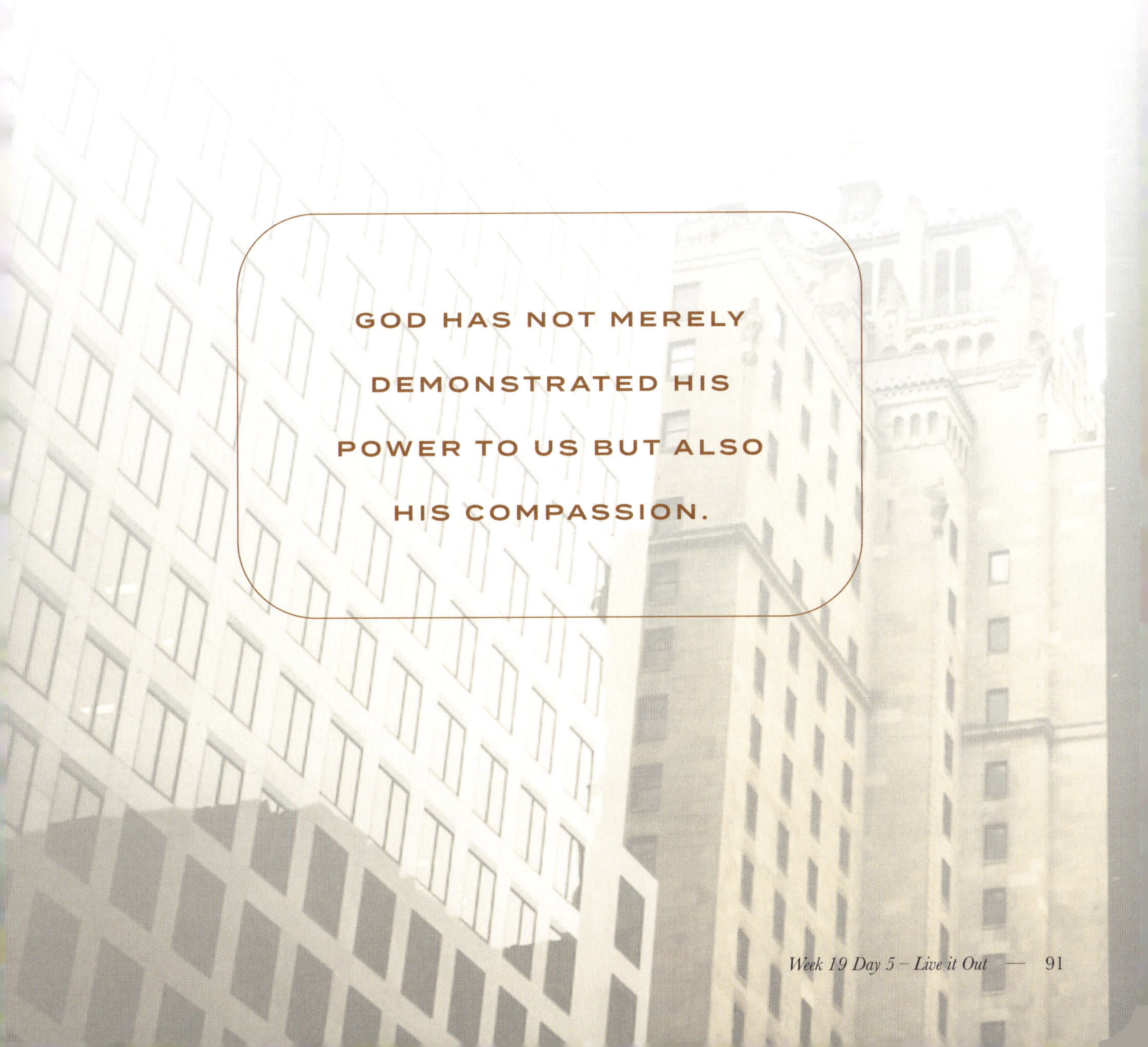

GOD HAS NOT MERELY DEMONSTRATED HIS POWER TO US BUT ALSO HIS COMPASSION.

Introduction

WEEK TWENTY

This week, we will explore the concept of heart circumcision as we look at Deuteronomy 30:6 and Romans 2:28–29. In doing so, we will learn how such heart circumcision can only be achieved through the transforming work of the Holy Spirit within us, which is given to us through faith in Christ Jesus.

MARK IT UP

Old Testament Passage

Today, we will study the idea of heart circumcision, first introduced by Moses in Deuteronomy 30:6 as he prepares the Israelites to enter into the Promised Land. Read Deuteronomy 30:6 multiple times and annotate, or mark up, the text as you read. For tips and examples on annotating, see page 196–207.

1. Highlight any words or phrases that point to Christ.

2. Make note of any attributes of God seen in the text.

3. Highlight the word "circumcise" in a different color, then look up and read Genesis 17:11–12. What does circumcision symbolize? How is it different in the context of Deuteronomy 30:6?

4. Circle the word "will" throughout this verse. What does this verb teach you about God's promise in this verse?

5. Underline the pronouns in this verse. Who are the "you" and the "your descendants" referring to?

6 Draw a box around any conjunctions (i.e., words such as *for*, *and*, *nor*, *but*, *or*, *yet*, *so*). in this passage. How might the idea of heart circumcision relate to loving God "with all your heart and all your soul"?

DEUTERONOMY 30:6

6 The LORD your God will circumcise your heart and the
hearts of your descendants, and you will love him with
all your heart and all your soul so that you will live.

Go Deeper

1 Read Deuteronomy 30:6.

To a modern reader, the concept of "heart circumcision" might be shrouded in confusion. And therefore, what Moses communicates through this passage can be difficult to understand without deeper context. As we seek to understand "heart circumcision," we must rewind the biblical narrative to the very first person who was ever circumcised—a person who received a promise that changed the course of human history.

2 Read Genesis 12:1–7. What does God promise to Abram?

With this promise, which eventually becomes known as the Abrahamic covenant, God promises to make Abram into a great nation and to bless all people of the earth through him (a promise that is confirmed in Genesis 15). However, at this time, Abram has no children. He is seventy-five years old and called by God to leave his homeland. The logistics of becoming a great nation do not seem to be falling into place. And yet, Abram trusts God's promise.

3 Read Genesis 17. Why does God command Abram to be circumcised?

Fourteen years later, Abram is still without the child promised through his wife, Sarai. But God has not forgotten Abram. In chapter 17, God appears again to Abram, changes his name to Abraham, and promises to multiply him greatly. His covenant love will remain with Abraham and his descendants. As a physical reminder of God's promise, God commands Abraham and all of his descendants to be circumcised, or to have their foreskin removed. Through this act, future generations will remember the covenant blessing of God; they will be set apart from neighboring nations as God's chosen people.

4 Now read Deuteronomy 29:16–30:20. What do these verses communicate about God's character?

While the Genesis passages display God's covenant love for Abraham and his descendants, Deuteronomy 29:16–29 describes the Israelites' inability to return the same steadfast love. They will abandon the covenant by breaking God's law (given in Exodus 20–23), bowing in worship to other Gods, and experiencing the fury of God's jealous wrath. But that is not the end of the story. Though the Israelites are unfaithful to God, God cannot break the promise He made to Abraham.

Moses, delivering the last of his speeches to the Israelites before they venture into the Promised Land, encourages the Israelites to return to God (Deuteronomy 30). If they return, God will multiply them, bring them back to the land, and circumcise their hearts. Sound familiar? He will fulfill the promises He made to Abraham.

However, the Israelites will never be able to keep God's law in their own strength. God Himself will fulfill His covenant. God will take this external sign of circumcision and apply it to their hearts. He will mark them as His own from within. God will take it upon Himself to change the hearts of His people so that they may finally love Him wholeheartedly.

Abrahamic covenant: God's promise to the patriarch Abram (later named Abraham) that initiated God's creation of the nation of Israel, through whom the Messiah would come and redeem the world from sin (Genesis 12:1–7, Genesis 15, Genesis 17).

MARK IT UP

New Testament Passage

Today, we will continue to trace the theme of heart circumcision as we look at Paul's words in Romans 2:28–29. Read the passage multiple times and annotate, or mark up, the text as you read. For tips and examples on annotating, see page 196–207.

1. Highlight any words or phrases that point to Christ.

2. Make note of any attributes of God seen in the text.

3. Read these verses in a few different translations. What differences in wording do you see? Note those differences.

4. Circle any instances of comparisons or contrasts that you see in these verses. What do these comparisons and contrasts teach you about true circumcision?

5. Underline the phrase "by the Spirit." Who completes the circumcision of the heart? Why is this important?

ROMANS 2:28–29

28 For a person is not a Jew who is one outwardly, and true
circumcision is not something visible in the flesh.
29 On the contrary, a person is a Jew who is one inwardly,
and circumcision is of the heart — by the Spirit, not the letter.
That person's praise is not from people but from God.

Make the Christ Connection

1 Read Deuteronomy 30:6 and Romans 2:25–29.

If you had to choose your last words to those you love, what would you say? In Deuteronomy 30, Moses shared some of his last words with the Israelites before they continued into the Promised Land without him. Moses pointed forward to a day when Israel would be brought into full obedience—a day when they would be marked as God's people, not with an external symbol but with an internal heart change.

2 According to Romans 2:25–29, what does heart circumcision enable a believer to do?

With circumcised hearts, God's people would finally worship their Savior wholeheartedly. Yet true heart circumcision would never be accomplished in their own strength. The Israelites would need another to be obedient in their place. They would need another to love God perfectly on their behalf.

3 Read Romans 2:25–29 again. How do these verses describe true circumcision?

As Paul writes to the Roman church, He proclaims what Moses pointed toward. The symbol of circumcision is just that—a symbol. Yes, this symbol marked the Jews as God's chosen people, but Paul reminds the Romans that this covenant symbol is rendered meaningless if God's people do not keep His law. And God's law is impossible for wayward sinners to keep.

Enter Jesus. Jesus kept God's law perfectly—never sinning and always fully obeying the Father. Jesus is the One whom the Old Testament sacrificial system pointed toward all along—He single-handedly completed the removal of sin by His sacrifice on the cross. Upon Jesus's death, He inaugurated a new Law in which He credits His perfect obedience to those who profess faith in Him. His perfection becomes the perfection of His people. And upon profession of this faith, those in Christ receive the Holy Spirit who indwells them, empowering them to turn from their sin and follow God—just as God's people were meant to do all along. This is true circumcision of the heart.

4 Read Romans 3:21–30. How do these verses level the distinction between Jews and Gentiles?

To first-century Jews who boasted in their circumcision, Paul's words were likely shocking and even insulting. Circumcision was a part of the Jewish identity, setting Jews apart from unbelieving Gentiles. Yet in Romans, Paul levels the playing field between Jews and Gentiles by asserting that all have sinned and fall short of the glory of God (Romans 3:23). External circumcision is no cause for boasting, for both Jews and Gentiles need Jesus in order to be counted righteous.

Therefore, the mark of a true Jew, or one of God's people, is not external circumcision or even obedience to the Law. The true mark of God's people is now the indwelling of the Holy Spirit. And through this indwelling, the hearts of God's people turn from stone to flesh (Ezekiel 36:26) and are enabled to obey Him in genuine love. Those indwelled with the Holy Spirit are God's true covenant community—the new Israel—marked by the very Spirit of God within them and set apart to proclaim Christ's gospel with the world.

External circumcision was always meant to communicate an internal reality—a heart that loves and obeys God. Jesus's sacrifice made this possible and abolished the need for physical circumcision.

5 Write a brief summary of what you have learned this week. Pray a prayer of thanksgiving to God for enabling us to walk in His ways by grace through faith.

Live it Out

1 Read Deuteronomy 30:6 and Romans 2:28–29.

Do you find yourself tempted to rely on your own strength rather than on God's strength? Like the Israelites, we need the reminder that it is only through Christ that we receive salvation and eternal life. Just as Paul warned the Jewish Christians against leaning on their Israelite heritage for salvation, we must remember that we have no reason to boast in our own abilities or our spiritual resumes. Our church attendance and Bible study participation do not earn our salvation.

Salvation does not depend upon our performance but upon the perfect life of Jesus—the perfect life that He obediently sacrificed on the cross for our sin. If you are in Christ today, your heart is circumcised—not by your accomplishments but by grace through faith in Jesus. Any good fruit that your life produces is the result of a heart made new by Christ. Therefore, Jesus deserves all of the glory and all of our praise.

REFLECT ON THIS WEEK'S VERSES AS YOU ANSWER THE FOLLOWING QUESTIONS.

2 Based on what you learned this week, how would you describe heart circumcision to a friend?

3 Read Ephesians 2:8–9. How are you tempted to believe that your salvation depends upon your works rather than upon grace?

4 Write a prayer, asking God to grow your love and obedience to Him by the power of the Holy Spirit within you.

JESUS DESERVES ALL OF THE GLORY AND ALL OF OUR PRAISE.

Tracing the Theme of Heart Circumcision

This week, we studied Deuteronomy 30:6 and Romans 2:28–29 as we traced the theme of heart circumcision through Scripture. But these are not the only biblical passages that discuss this concept. Below, you will find a sampling of verses that speak to our need for heart circumcision and the way God has graciously met that need through Jesus Christ.

DEUTERONOMY 10:16

Therefore, circumcise your hearts and don't be stiff-necked any longer.

DEUTERONOMY 30:6

The Lord your God will circumcise your heart and the hearts of your descendants, and you will love him with all your heart and all your soul so that you will live.

JEREMIAH 4:4

Circumcise yourselves to the Lord; remove the foreskin of your hearts, men of Judah and residents of Jerusalem. Otherwise, my wrath will break out like fire and burn with no one to extinguish it because of your evil deeds.

JEREMIAH 9:25–26

Look, the days are coming — this is the LORD's declaration — when I will punish all the circumcised yet uncircumcised: Egypt, Judah, Edom, the Ammonites, Moab, and all the inhabitants of the desert who clip the hair on their temples. All these nations are uncircumcised, and the whole house of Israel is uncircumcised in heart.

ROMANS 2:28–29

For a person is not a Jew who is one outwardly, and true circumcision is not something visible in the flesh. On the contrary, a person is a Jew who is one inwardly, and circumcision is of the heart — by the Spirit, not the letter. That person's praise is not from people but from God.

COLOSSIANS 2:11

You were also circumcised in him with a circumcision not done with hands, by putting off the body of flesh, in the circumcision of Christ.

Introduction

WEEK TWENTY-ONE

This week, we will look at the theme of rest—how God provided it to the Israelites in Joshua 21:43–45 by bringing them into the land of Canaan and how Jesus leads us to an even greater rest as described in Hebrews 4:5–11. By dwelling on the rest we currently enjoy as Christians and the rest that is still to come, we will be encouraged to persevere when life becomes difficult.

MARK IT UP

Old Testament Passage

Today, we will begin the week by studying Joshua 21:43–45—a short passage that describes the Israelites' arrival in the Promised Land after forty years of wandering in the wilderness. Read the passage multiple times and annotate, or mark up, the text as you read. For tips and examples on annotating, see page 196–207.

1. Highlight any words or phrases that point to Christ.

2. Make note of any attributes of God seen in the text.

3. Circle repeated words that you see in these verses.

4. Underline words or phrases that speak of God's faithfulness to His promises.

5. How do these verses emphasize Israel's security in their new homeland?

6. Why was the land important? What promises is God keeping by bringing Israel into it?

JOSHUA 21:43–45

43 So the LORD gave Israel all the land he had sworn to give their
ancestors, and they took possession of it and settled there.
44 The LORD gave them rest on every side according to all he
had sworn to their ancestors. None of their enemies were
able to stand against them, for the LORD handed over all their
enemies to them. 45 None of the good promises the LORD had
made to the house of Israel failed. Everything was fulfilled.

Go Deeper

1 Read Joshua 21:43–45.

When it comes to understanding the Bible, it is difficult to overstate the importance of God's promises to Abraham in Genesis 12:1–3. In that passage, God promised to give Abraham numerous descendants as well as the land of Canaan for his descendants to live in. And through Abraham's family, God promised that He would bring blessing to all nations.

True to His promise, God multiplied the people of Israel—Abraham's descendants—while they lived in Egypt. (In fact, it was their very numbers that caused Pharaoh to feel threatened by them and to enslave them in Exodus 1:8–13). And while the Israelites were captive in Egypt, God—true to His promise of bringing them into Canaan—sent Moses to confront Pharaoh and bring Israel out of Egypt (Exodus 6:2–8).

But the journey from Egypt to Canaan was anything but smooth, as illustrated by what happened at the place referred to as both Meribah and Massah.

2 Read Psalm 95:8–11, which talks about the generation of Israelites who came out of Egypt. What does this passage say they did? How did God respond?

After the Israelites left Meribah and approached Canaan, Moses sent twelve men to spy out the land for forty days. One thing that all the spies could agree on was that the land was indeed wonderful. It was "flowing with milk and honey" and was an "extremely good land" (Numbers 13:27, 14:7). For ten of the spies, however, the land's current inhabitants seemed too strong for them to defeat in battle, and in response, the Israelite community suggested turning around and heading back to Egypt. Joshua and Caleb—the other two spies—took a very different view, claiming that since God was with them, they had nothing to fear. Since God had promised this land to them, it would be rebellion against Him to give up and turn back (Numbers 13:26–14:9). But sadly, the people of Israel chose to rebel against God.

The consequence for their rebellion was that the older Israelites were forbidden from entering the land—or, as Psalm 95:11 describes it, God's "rest." Instead, the younger Israelites would enjoy that privilege. As the book of Joshua opens, the older generation has passed away, and the younger generation—now led by Joshua—is ready to enter the land.

3 Read Joshua 1:1–9. What does God assure Joshua of in these verses? On what will Israel's success in battle depend?

To some of the spies, the Israelites seemed like grasshoppers compared to the Canaanites (Numbers 13:33). But what God reminds Joshua of in Joshua 1—and what is repeatedly demonstrated throughout the book—is that Israel's security will be found in trusting Him. So, as long as God is with them, nothing that stands against them will succeed.

Sure enough, the book of Joshua records how Israel conquered the land of Canaan. And near the end is the summary statement, reiterating that God kept all His promises to Israel, that He gave them victory in battle, and that He gave them rest (Joshua 21:43–45).

4 Read Psalm 20:7. How does the book of Joshua demonstrate the truth of this verse?

Meribah: Hebrew word meaning "quarreling" and the name given to the location in the wilderness where Israel complained about their lack of water in Exodus 17:1–7. This same location is also referred to as Massah ("testing") in Exodus 17:7. For the author of Psalm 95, this moment summarizes Israel's demeanor in the wilderness, which culminated in their not being allowed to enter the land.

MARK IT UP

New Testament Passage

Today, we will continue to study the theme of rest throughout Scripture by looking at Hebrews 4:5–11. In doing so, we will begin to see how we can find true rest in Christ alone. Read the passage multiple times and annotate, or mark up, the text as you read. For tips and examples on annotating, see page 196–207.

1. Highlight any words or phrases that point to Christ.

2. Make note of any attributes of God seen in the text.

3. Circle repeated words.

4. Underline any references you see to Old Testament passages we looked at on Day 2 of this week. (Hint: If you need help identifying these Old Testament passages, we recommend looking up Hebrews 4:5–11 in a Bible that provides cross-references or an online tool, such as Bible Gateway.)

5. Why do you think the author is writing this passage? Based on verse 11, what kind of impact should the preceding verses have on the lives of the readers?

HEBREWS 4:5–11

5 Again, in that passage he says, They will never enter my rest.
6 Therefore, since it remains for some to enter it, and those
who formerly received the good news did not enter because
of disobedience, 7 he again specifies a certain day — today.
He specified this speaking through David after such a long time:

> Today, if you hear his voice, do not harden your hearts.

8 For if Joshua had given them rest, God would not have spoken
later about another day. 9 Therefore, a Sabbath rest remains
for God's people. 10 For the person who has entered his rest
has rested from his own works, just as God did from his.
11 Let us, then, make every effort to enter that rest, so that
no one will fall into the same pattern of disobedience.

Make the Christ Connection

1 Read Joshua 21:43–45 and Hebrews 4:1–11.

According to its unknown author, the book of Hebrews is a "message of exhortation" (Hebrews 13:22) for its original audience. It is like a written-out sermon meant to encourage Jewish Christians experiencing trials as a result of following Jesus. They have already gone through seasons of trial in the past and endured them joyfully (Hebrews 10:32–34). But they are facing some new trials (Hebrews 10:35–39), and based on the author's consistent encouragement to persevere, they may be getting worn down. They may even be wondering if continuing to follow Jesus is worth the trouble.

2 What trials have you experienced as a result of being a Christian? Have you ever found yourself wondering if following Jesus is worth it?

The book of Hebrews is full of exhortations meant to help its original readers persevere in their faith. One of those exhortations flows out of a comparison the author makes between Jesus and Moses. Like Jesus, Moses was faithful to God. But Moses was merely a servant *in* God's house. Jesus, on the other hand, is God's Son, who is *over* God's house (Hebrews 3:1–6). In other words, Jesus is similar—yet far superior—to Moses.

And this prompts the author to reflect on the similarities between those who followed Moses and those who follow Jesus. He warns his readers against following in the footsteps of the Israelites, who, when faced with difficulties (such as the report of the spies), wanted to give up following Moses and turn back to slavery in Egypt. So now, as the those reading this letter face difficulties, they should press on in following Jesus.

3. While they were in the wilderness, the Israelites had Egypt behind them and the Promised Land of Canaan ahead of them. In what ways is our experience as Christians similar to theirs? What lies behind us? What lies ahead?

Psalm 95 is crucial for the author's point in Hebrews 3–4. Specifically, verses 7–11 of that psalm are an appeal to not repeat the sins which kept many Israelites from entering God's "rest" (i.e., the Promised Land). That the psalmist is saying this "today" (Psalm 95:7)—to Israelites who had already been living in the land for centuries—communicates an important point: simply dwelling in Canaan did not mean that they had "arrived." Canaan was always meant to point to a deeper rest God wants for His people, one which cannot be achieved by merely dwelling in an "extremely good land" (Numbers 14:7).

The true rest God provides for His people is ultimately not found in the land of Canaan but in the person of Jesus. Through His death and resurrection, we have been set free from slavery to sin and death and are being led through the wilderness of this world—with all its difficulties—to our new homeland: a new earth, where we will dwell in the presence of God forever (Revelation 21:1–4).

4. Spend time asking God to help you persevere in hard times and remind you of the rest that lies before you.

Live it Out

1 Read Joshua 21:43–45 and Hebrews 4:5–11.

Joshua played an instrumental role in Israel's history, leading the people into the "rest" of Canaan. But as Hebrews 4 makes clear, simply dwelling in Canaan was not the point. The point was to dwell *with God* in Canaan. To enter God's presence is to enter true, lasting rest.

As Christians, there is a sense in which we already enjoy this rest. For example, Jesus promises rest to all who come to Him (Matthew 11:28). And because He died for our sins, we presently have "peace with God" (Romans 5:1).

But there is a measure of rest still to come for us. Just as Joshua led the Israelites into the land of Canaan, Jesus is leading us to not only a new *land* but a whole new *earth* (Isaiah 65:17, 66:22; Revelation 21:1–4). There, we will enjoy true rest as we live in God's presence in a world free from sin and death. With such an "extremely good land" ahead of us, let us press on through the difficulties of this world and strive to enter it.

REFLECT ON THIS WEEK'S VERSES AS YOU ANSWER THE FOLLOWING QUESTIONS.

2 Imagine going back to the moment when the Israelites were disheartened about entering the land and wondering if they should turn back (Numbers 13:26–14:9). What would you say to reassure them? What reminders do you think they would need to hear?

3 As Christians currently living in a fallen world, what reminders do you need to hear in order to continue striving toward God's rest?

4 Read Hebrews 3:12–14. As we strive to enter God's rest, what role do other believers play? How can you fulfill this role in the lives of others?

TO ENTER GOD'S PRESENCE IS TO ENTER TRUE, LASTING REST.

Introduction

WEEK TWENTY-TWO

This week, we will read Judges 2:10–19 and Romans 6:15–23 and learn how Jesus gives us true freedom by releasing us from the cycle of sinful living. In response, you will be encouraged to serve and obey the Lord in response to the freedom you have received through Christ.

JESUS GIVES US TRUE FREEDOM BY RELEASING US FROM THE CYCLE OF SINFUL LIVING.

MARK IT UP

Old Testament Passage

Today, we will begin to learn about the Israelites' pattern of sinful living by studying Judges 2:10–19. This will set us up to better understand the true freedom from our sin that Jesus gives us, which we will look at later in the week. For now, read Judges 2:10–19 two or three times and annotate, or mark up, the text as you read. For tips and examples on annotating, see page 196–207.

1. Highlight any words or phrases that point to Christ.

2. Make note of any attributes of God seen in the text.

3. Underline what the Israelites do wrong in this passage. How would you sum up the Israelites' sin, according to the text?

4. Circle any verbs—or action words—related to God. How does God respond to the Israelites' sin?

5. What occurs for the Israelites while a judge is alive, and what is the Israelites' response when a judge dies?

10 That whole generation was also gathered to their
ancestors. After them another generation rose up who
did not know the Lord or the works he had done for Israel.
11 The Israelites did what was evil in the Lord's sight. They
worshiped the Baals 12 and abandoned the Lord, the God of
their ancestors, who had brought them out of Egypt. They
followed other gods from the surrounding peoples and
bowed down to them. They angered the Lord, 13 for they
abandoned him and worshiped Baal and the Ashtoreths.
14 The Lord's anger burned against Israel, and he handed
them over to marauders who raided them. He sold them
to the enemies around them, and they could no longer
resist their enemies. 15 Whenever the Israelites went
out, the Lord was against them and brought disaster on
them, just as he had promised and sworn to them. So they

suffered greatly. 16 The LORD raised up judges, who saved
them from the power of their marauders, 17 but they did not
listen to their judges. Instead, they prostituted themselves
with other gods, bowing down to them. They quickly
turned from the way of their ancestors, who had walked in
obedience to the LORD's commands. They did not do as their
ancestors did. 18 Whenever the LORD raised up a judge for
the Israelites, the LORD was with him and saved the people
from the power of their enemies while the judge was still
alive. The LORD was moved to pity whenever they groaned
because of those who were oppressing and afflicting them.
19 Whenever the judge died, the Israelites would act even
more corruptly than their ancestors, following other gods
to serve them and bow in worship to them. They did not
turn from their evil practices or their obstinate ways.

Go Deeper

1 Read Judges 2:10–19.

There are many movies that depict someone living the same day over again. While the main character tries to do different things each day, they find themselves waking up and having to relive that same day, encountering the same experiences again and again. Over time, they realize that there is something particular they must do to break themselves out of this cycle. In the book of Judges, the Israelites find themselves in a similar situation. Although they are not reliving the same day over and over again, they are in a cycle of sinful living—and there is nothing they can do on their own to break themselves free.

But how did the Israelites find themselves in this place? After Moses died, Joshua took over leadership. The Israelites had remained obedient to the Lord under Joshua's leadership—but all of this changed when Joshua died. We see this clearly in the first chapter of Judges. God had commanded the Israelites to remove all the Canaanites from the land (Deuteronomy 7:1–6). And while some tribes did fight and remove the Canaanites, the rest of the tribes failed to fully obey God's command. Their failure to obey God is what contributes to the wickedness we see in Judges 2. Because they did not drive out the Canaanites, the Israelites now have people among them who do not worship God, and their pagan worship negatively affects Israel, contributing to their apostasy.

2 Read Joshua 23:6–8. How do we see the Israelites fail to listen to these words from Joshua? What should they have done?

God's response is appropriate and fair in light of the Israelites' behavior. God has brought the Israelites out of slavery and into Canaan, where they will make their home. He has blessed them, provided for them, and fought on their behalf. But the Israelites have turned away from Him, so much so that they have abandoned Him. They utterly disobey God's commands to worship Him alone (Deuteronomy 6:4–5), and they instead bow down to the false gods around them. Therefore, it is just and right for God to punish them for their sin.

3 Read Joshua 23:12–13, 16. In what ways do you see these words come true in Judges 2:10–19? Why do you think Israel did not listen to this warning?

Even though God punishes Israel, He remains gracious to them by raising up judges who bring about help and salvation for the Israelites. Sadly, Israel does not listen to these judges (Judges 2:17), yet they are saved from their enemies as long as the judge lives. Unfortunately, however, the Israelites only continue in sin once the judge dies. God has been gracious to Israel despite their sin, but they remain in their rebellion, therefore keeping themselves in a pattern of sinful living. Even still, God will remain gracious to Israel, making a way for One to come who will save them and completely set them free.

4 Praise God for the ways He remains gracious even when you fail to give Him the worship He deserves.

apostasy: Abandoning and rejecting the Lord.

JESUS SETS US FREE

FROM BONDAGE TO SIN.

MARK IT UP

New Testament Passage

After studying Judges 2:10–19 to see the cycle of sin that the Israelites continually found themselves in, we will now turn to Paul's words in the book of Romans to see how Jesus sets us free from bondage to sin. Read Romans 6:15–23 two or three times and annotate, or mark up, the text as you read. For tips and examples on annotating, see page 196–207.

1. Highlight any words or phrases that point to Christ.

2. Make note of any attributes of God seen in the text.

3. Circle the phrase "so now" in verse 19. What type of slaves were we before Christ, and what types of slaves are we now that we are in Christ?

4. Underline the outcome of being a slave of unrighteousness (verse 21) and then underline the outcome of being a slave of righteousness (verse 22). What are the different outcomes?

5. What are believers set free from according to this passage?

ROMANS 6:15–23

15 What then? Should we sin because we are not under the
law but under grace? Absolutely not! 16 Don't you know that
if you offer yourselves to someone as obedient slaves, you
are slaves of that one you obey—either of sin leading to
death or of obedience leading to righteousness? 17 But thank
God that, although you used to be slaves of sin, you obeyed
from the heart that pattern of teaching to which you were
handed over, 18 and having been set free from sin, you
became enslaved to righteousness. 19 I am using a human
analogy because of the weakness of your flesh. For just as

you offered the parts of yourselves as slaves to impurity,
and to greater and greater lawlessness, so now offer them
as slaves to righteousness, which results in sanctification.
20 For when you were slaves of sin, you were free with
regard to righteousness. 21 So what fruit was produced
then from the things you are now ashamed of? The outcome
of those things is death. 22 But now, since you have been
set free from sin and have become enslaved to God, you
have your fruit, which results in sanctification — and the
outcome is eternal life! 23 For the wages of sin is death,
but the gift of God is eternal life in Christ Jesus our Lord.

Make the Christ Connection

1 Read Judges 2:10–19 and Romans 6:15–23.

The Israelites were stuck in a cycle of continuous sinful living. Even when they repented and turned to God, they found themselves falling back into sin and turning away from God once again. The Israelites' experience in this is each one of our own experiences, as well. Because of the Fall, we are all enslaved to sin. Sin controls us, and there is nothing we can do on our own to release ourselves from sin's grip. Thankfully, out of God's great mercy and grace, He has given us Jesus Christ, who gives us complete freedom from sin.

This truth is powerfully proclaimed in Romans 6:15–23. So far in the book of Romans, Paul has been unpacking the gospel and our need for Jesus, and in chapter 6, he describes the new life that we receive in Christ. He explains that because we have been saved by Christ, we no longer choose to live in sin but to obey the Lord instead. It is precisely because Jesus has brought us from death to life and released us from sin that we live for the Lord and obey Him.

2 Read Romans 6:6–7, 11. What does Paul say has happened to us as believers, according to these verses? What should be our response?

Being dead to sin and alive to God in Christ means that we have a new allegiance (Galatians 2:20). No longer do we live for ourselves. No longer do we allow sin to control us. Because Jesus has set us free from slavery to sin and released us from the cycle of sinful living, we live for Him. We strive to walk in obedience to Him rather than walking in willful sin and disobedience (Romans 6:12).

Paul presses this point further by drawing a distinction between two different kinds of slavery (Romans 6:19–22). Before Christ, we are considered slaves to sin. In Christ, we are slaves to righteousness. Being a slave to impurity results in death; being a slave to righteousness results in sanctification and eternal life. As believers, we have been made slaves to righteousness because of Christ, and we experience transformation and life because of this new reality.

3 How does the transformation and life we receive through Christ impact our obedience to the Lord?

Paul's language of "slavery" would be impactful to the Roman audience to whom he is writing. While many Roman slaves became slaves unwillingly, others chose to become slaves. In doing so, they accepted that they were losing their freedom by enslaving themselves to another. In a similar way, we give up our freedom (living for ourselves) to become servants of Christ, acknowledging that we now live for the Lord when we accept Him as our Savior. Yet there is no one greater to whom we could be enslaved, not only because He is our compassionate Father but also because through our relationship with God, given to us through Christ, we receive true freedom (John 8:36, Galatians 5:1).

Being a slave to righteousness is a beautiful thing because it means that we have been set free from sin. We no longer walk in continual unrighteousness toward an end that results in eternal punishment. The freedom we have in Christ changes our trajectory and gives us life everlasting.

4 Thank Jesus for releasing you from the cycle of sin and ask Him to help you respond to His great salvation through joyful obedience to Him.

Live it Out

1 Read Judges 2:10–19 and Romans 6:15–23.

Jesus's salvation sets us free from slavery to sin and breaks us from the cycle of sinful living. And because Jesus released us and set us free, we live for Him. But what does this look like practically? It looks like seeking to obey God and serve Him in all that we do. It involves resisting and confessing our sin with the help of the Spirit, rather than yielding to temptation (Romans 6:12–13). It means that we desire to worship and be faithful to the Lord in light of the incredible salvation we have received through Christ.

And when being a slave of righteousness feels hard or complicated, we can set our eyes on the gospel. Fixing our eyes on the gospel reminds us of how Jesus rescued us from sin and gave us salvation and eternal life (Colossians 1:13–14). Such truth encourages us in our fight against sin and our obedience to the Lord. The gospel also reminds us of how we do not have to feel like sin has power over us. Because Jesus has set us free from sin and given us the power of the Spirit within us if we have accepted Christ, we are able to resist sin and live as joyful servants of the Lord.

Jesus is the One who provides ultimate salvation. He is the ultimate leader whom God raised up to save us. And because of Christ's sacrifice, we have assurance that even when we sin, we have eternal salvation and the promise that we have been forgiven.

REFLECT ON THIS WEEK'S VERSES AS YOU ANSWER THE FOLLOWING QUESTIONS.

2 How does the freedom Jesus gives you from sin impact the way you view your sin?

3 What does it look like for you to live as a slave of righteousness in your daily life?

4 In what ways can you rely on the Spirit to help you live as a slave of righteousness?

JESUS IS THE ONE WHO PROVIDES ULTIMATE SALVATION.

The Judges Cycle

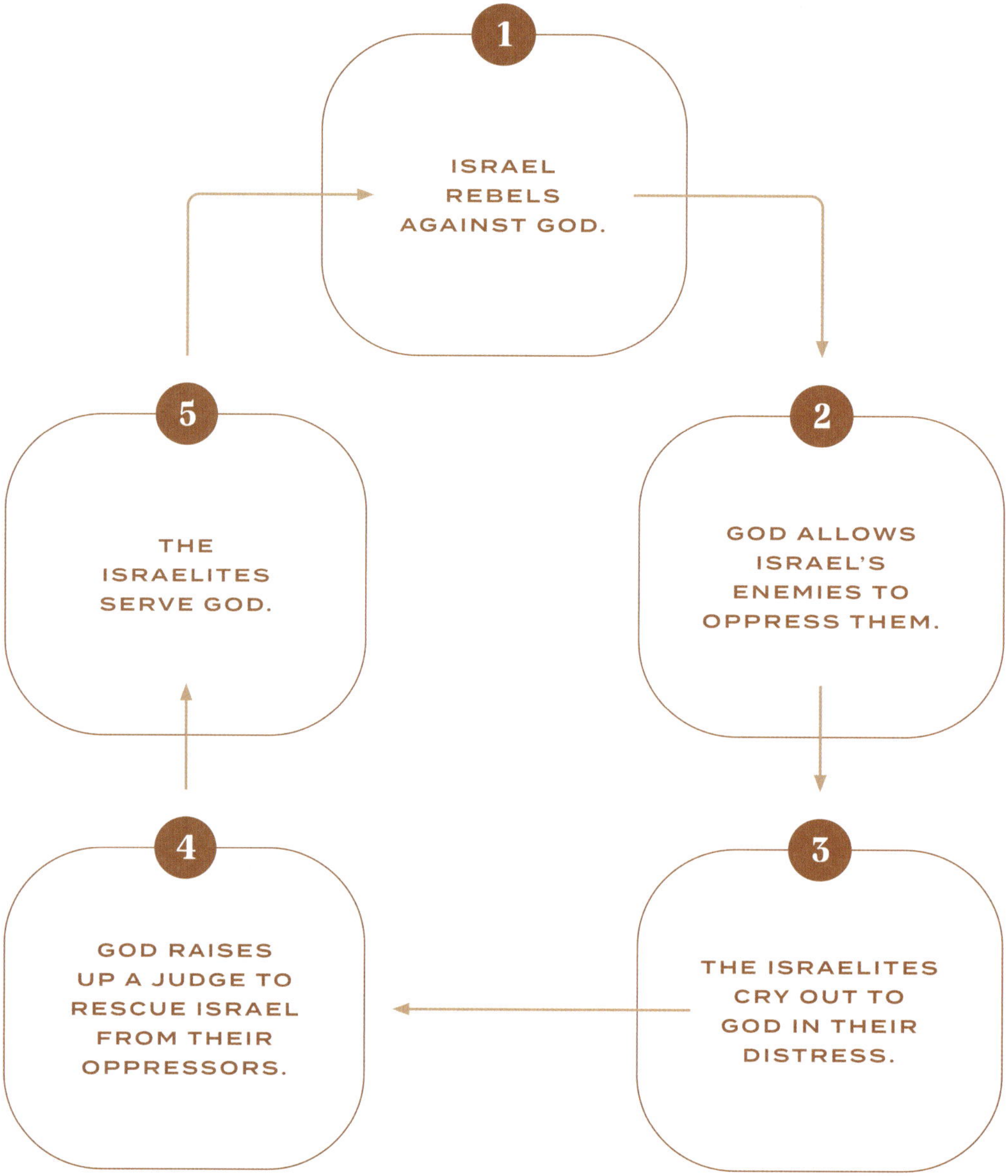

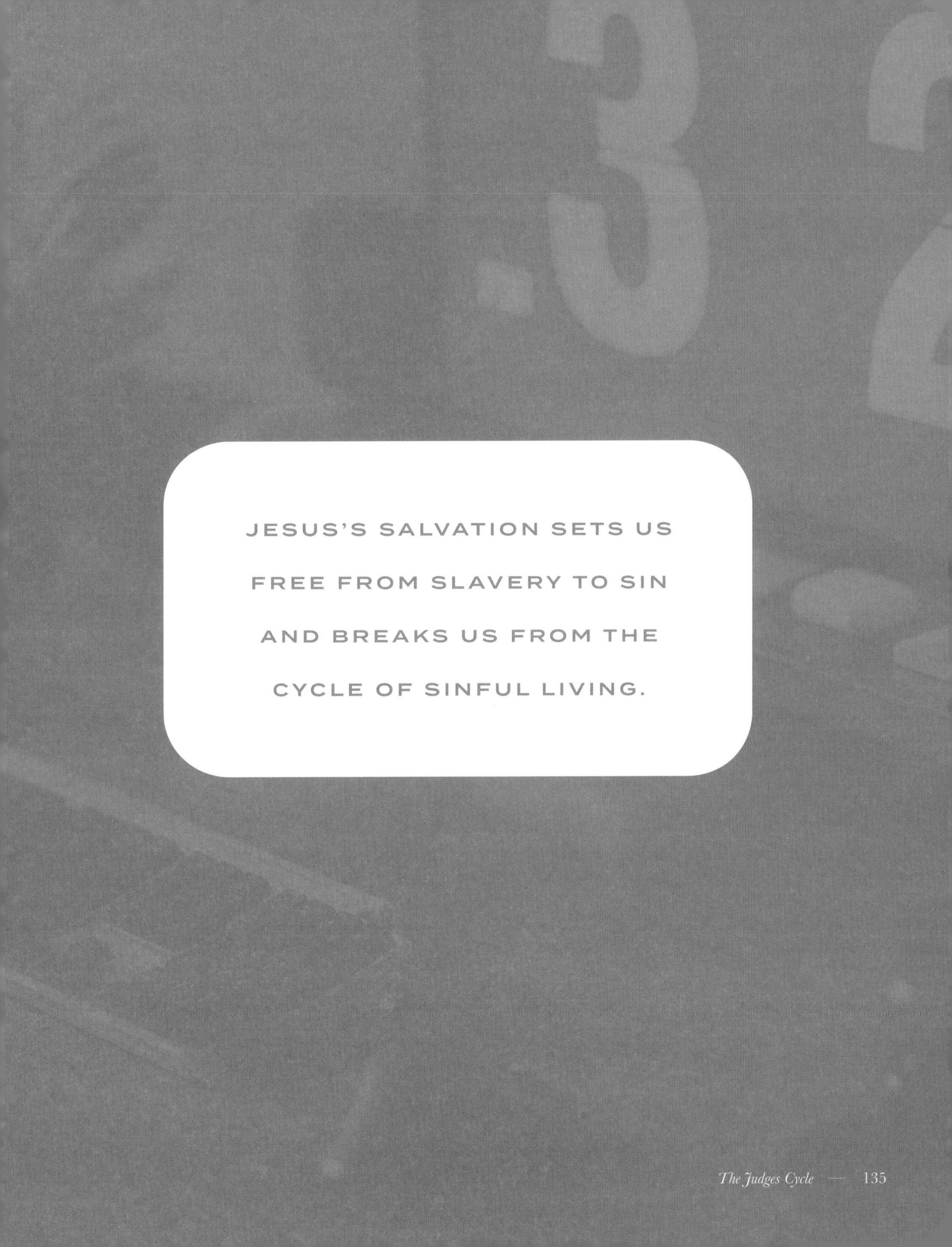

JESUS'S SALVATION SETS US FREE FROM SLAVERY TO SIN AND BREAKS US FROM THE CYCLE OF SINFUL LIVING.

Introduction

WEEK TWENTY-THREE

This week, we will learn that Jesus is our true Redeemer as we trace the themes of redemption and provision through Ruth 4:14–15 and John 10:10. We will be encouraged to trust in Jesus during times of defenselessness and need, and we will be challenged to rejoice in God's abundant redemption from sin.

MARK IT UP

Old Testament Passage

Today, we will begin studying Ruth 4:14–15—two verses that come toward the end of the book of Ruth and help summarize the main point of this book. This will set us up well to explore Jesus's role as our Redeemer later in the week. To start, read Ruth 4:14–15 two or three times and annotate, or mark up, the text as you read. For tips and examples on annotating, see page 196–207.

1 Highlight any words or phrases that point to Christ.

2 Make note of any attributes of God seen in the text.

3 Circle the word "redeemer." In what ways does God redeem Ruth and Naomi from the grief and hardship brought upon them by the death of their husbands?*

4 Underline the word "life." How does God sustain Ruth and Naomi's lives through Boaz's kindness?

5 Make note of any references to God's actions in the text.

*Hint: For help answering this question, read through the previous chapters in the book of Ruth.

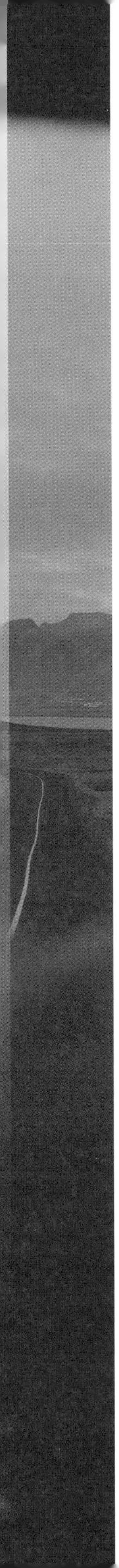

RUTH 4:14–15

14 The women said to Naomi, "Blessed be the Lord, who has not
left you without a family redeemer today. May his name become
well known in Israel. 15 He will renew your life and sustain you
in your old age. Indeed, your daughter-in-law, who loves you
and is better to you than seven sons, has given birth to him."

Go Deeper

1 Read Ruth 2, 4:14–15.

Life has a way of bringing about sudden changes. This is where Naomi and her daughters-in-law, Ruth and Orpah, find themselves as the book of Ruth opens. A famine has swept through the land and does not spare the three women's husbands. Each of them is widowed, facing the difficult decision of what to do next, and Naomi insists that the two young women return to their own families and their own land. Orpah makes the difficult choice to depart from Ruth and Naomi, but Ruth cannot bring herself to go. Instead, she pledges to Naomi that she will not leave her. As Naomi departs for her native land and family, Ruth—in a radical act of loyalty—goes with her.

The narrative follows Naomi and Ruth and shows us how God provides for them in the midst of tragedy and uncertainty. When the two women arrive in Naomi's homeland, Ruth begins to glean in the field of a man named Boaz, who shows kindness to Ruth, allowing her to gather food from his field and protecting her from anyone who might wish to do her harm (Ruth 2:8–9). Boaz will be the key vessel God uses to protect and provide for Ruth and Naomi.

Through conversing with Naomi, Ruth discovers that Boaz, through God's providence, is a kinsman-redeemer in Ruth's family (Ruth 2:19–20). The kinsman-redeemer has the responsibility of marrying a deceased family member's widow in order to care and provide for her. Boaz's kindness extends to Ruth once again, and he agrees to marry Ruth (Ruth 3:10–13, 4:9–10). Together, the two have a son named Obed (Ruth 4:13). Not only is Obed a blessing to Ruth and Boaz, but he will be able to care for Naomi as she ages, and Naomi is now able to mother again after the loss of her sons (Ruth 4:14–15).

2 How does the book of Ruth point to God's desire to love and care for us?

3 How has God providentially shown up in your life by providing in ways that only He can?

The book of Ruth ends with a short genealogy of those who came before and after Ruth and Boaz's son, Obed. It is here that we see that Obed is the grandfather of King David (Ruth 4:17, 22), the one to whom God would covenantally promise an eternal heir to his throne (2 Samuel 7). From the line of David would come our promised Messiah, Jesus Christ.

Jesus's love, devotion, and care for us is foreshadowed by Boaz's role as kinsman-redeemer. In Christ we have our own true and better Kinsman-Redeemer. Just as God did not leave Ruth and Naomi without a redeemer, nor has He left us without a Savior.

4 Write a prayer of gratitude, thanking God for His work in redemptive history.

glean: A practice in ancient Israel that allowed those who were poor to harvest leftover crops from the fields. God, in His Law, required land owners to not harvest their fields fully but to leave some behind, demonstrating His care for the poor and needy. See Leviticus 19:9–10.

providence: The ways in which God orchestrates all things for His divine purposes.

MARK IT UP

New Testament Passage

Now that we have studied the role of a kinsman-redeemer in the book of Ruth, we will turn to the book of John to see how Jesus is our true Redeemer. Read John 10:10 two or three times and annotate, or mark up, the text as you read. For tips and examples on annotating, see page 196–207.

1. Highlight any words or phrases that point to Christ.

2. Make note of any attributes of God seen in the text.

3. Circle the word "life" where it appears in the verse.

4. Underline the word in the verse that is used to describe the kind of life that Jesus gives. Use a dictionary to look up this word and then write the definition somewhere in the margin. Who is speaking in this verse, and who are they speaking to?

JOHN 10:10

10 A thief comes only to steal and kill and destroy. I have
come so that they may have life and have it in abundance.

Make the Christ Connection

1 Read Ruth 4:14–15 and John 10:7–15.

So far, we have seen how God providentially worked in the lives of Ruth and Naomi, giving them a son and a grandson, an heir, and an ancestor to King David (Ruth 4:14–17). In today's passage, we will see how another one of their descendants, Jesus, is the true and better Kinsman-Redeemer.

In John 10:7–14, Jesus addresses spiritual blindness after healing a blind man and being questioned by the Pharisees. The Pharisees are perplexed and angered at the manner by which this man who has been blind since birth has now been healed and is able to see. They are upset that he has been healed on a Sabbath (John 9:14, 16) and that he has been healed by Jesus, whose ministry they opposed (John 9:22, 28–29). When the formerly blind man expresses praise for the One who healed him, the religious leaders expel the man from the synagogue. When Jesus hears this and finds the man, Jesus reveals to him that He is, indeed, the Messiah. The man who was previously blind not only receives physical sight but also spiritual sight this day.

2 John 10:11–15. How does Jesus care and provide for us spiritually?

The religious leaders cared very little for the blind man who had been healed. Their only concern was to discredit Jesus and prove themselves to be the religious elite. Yet Jesus returns to the man in an act of divine care. Jesus calls Himself the Good Shepherd, who is known and followed by His sheep. He proclaims that unlike a thief who has come to steal, kill, and destroy, He has come so that His sheep may have abundant life. Those who place their faith in Jesus are His sheep, and He commits Himself to their well-being.

3 How does Jesus give us abundant life?

Not only does Jesus provide and care for us in our need, but He also protects us from false shepherds who intend to do us harm. Just as Boaz protected Ruth from the men in the field who may have wished to take advantage of her, Jesus stands in our defense and triumphs over the enemy who wishes us ruin.

However, Jesus does for us what Boaz never could have done. Through Jesus's righteous life, sacrificial death, and victorious resurrection, He is able to save us and the whole world from the penalty of sin—death. Jesus emptied Himself and took the form of a servant so that He could provide for both our physical and spiritual needs (Philippians 2:7–8). Because of Jesus, we can experience both abundant life here in the present and eternal life in the presence of God, face to face. Jesus is the true and better Boaz, committed to caring for us in our weak and vulnerable state—physically and spiritually—and saving us while we were still sinners.

4 Reflect on the ways that you are protected and cared for in Christ. Take some time to pray and thank God for sending Jesus as your great Redeemer.

Live it Out

1 Read Ruth 4:14–15 and John 10:10.

Inevitably, there will be times in our lives when we feel defenseless or when we have a difficult decision to make. Though we might feel, for a moment, that we are alone—without hope and without help—we can look to Jesus. Like Ruth, we are dependent on a kinsman-redeemer to redeem us. Christ—our Kinsman-Redeemer—died for us in order to save us from our sin and be near to us in times of trouble. While we deserve condemnation for our sin, Jesus promises to give us life abundantly.

Boaz was obedient to the law of God by agreeing to assume the role of redeemer on Ruth's behalf, caring and providing for her. Like Boaz did for Ruth, Christ's faithful obedience provides care and provision for us who place our faith in Him. Jesus came in the likeness of man so that He could redeem us from sin and provide for our needs. Jesus takes up our cause and becomes our Protector and Defender. Just as we can praise God for sending Jesus to be the true and better Redeemer when we were hopelessly enslaved to sin, we can also trust in Jesus to take up our cause and defend us—in redeeming us from sin and when we face opposition and trouble in our lives.

REFLECT ON THIS WEEK'S VERSES AS YOU ANSWER THE FOLLOWING QUESTIONS.

2 In what areas in your life do you need to trust Christ's care and provision?

3 Read John 3:16–17. How is Christ's obedience a blessing to us?

4 Take a moment to pray, asking God to care for your needs and thanking Him for being a faithful Provider.

CHRIST — OUR KINSMAN-REDEEMER — DIED FOR US IN ORDER TO SAVE US FROM OUR SIN AND BE NEAR TO US IN TIMES OF TROUBLE.

Introduction

WEEK TWENTY-FOUR

This week, you will read the prayer of Hannah in 1 Samuel 2:1–10 and the words of Mary in Luke 1:46–55. Through these passages, you will learn that Jesus came to the earth to humble the proud and to exalt the lowly, the humble, and those who feel shame. Through these passages, you will be encouraged by how Christ demonstrates God's good character and His heart for you, and you will be challenged to find all your satisfaction in Him.

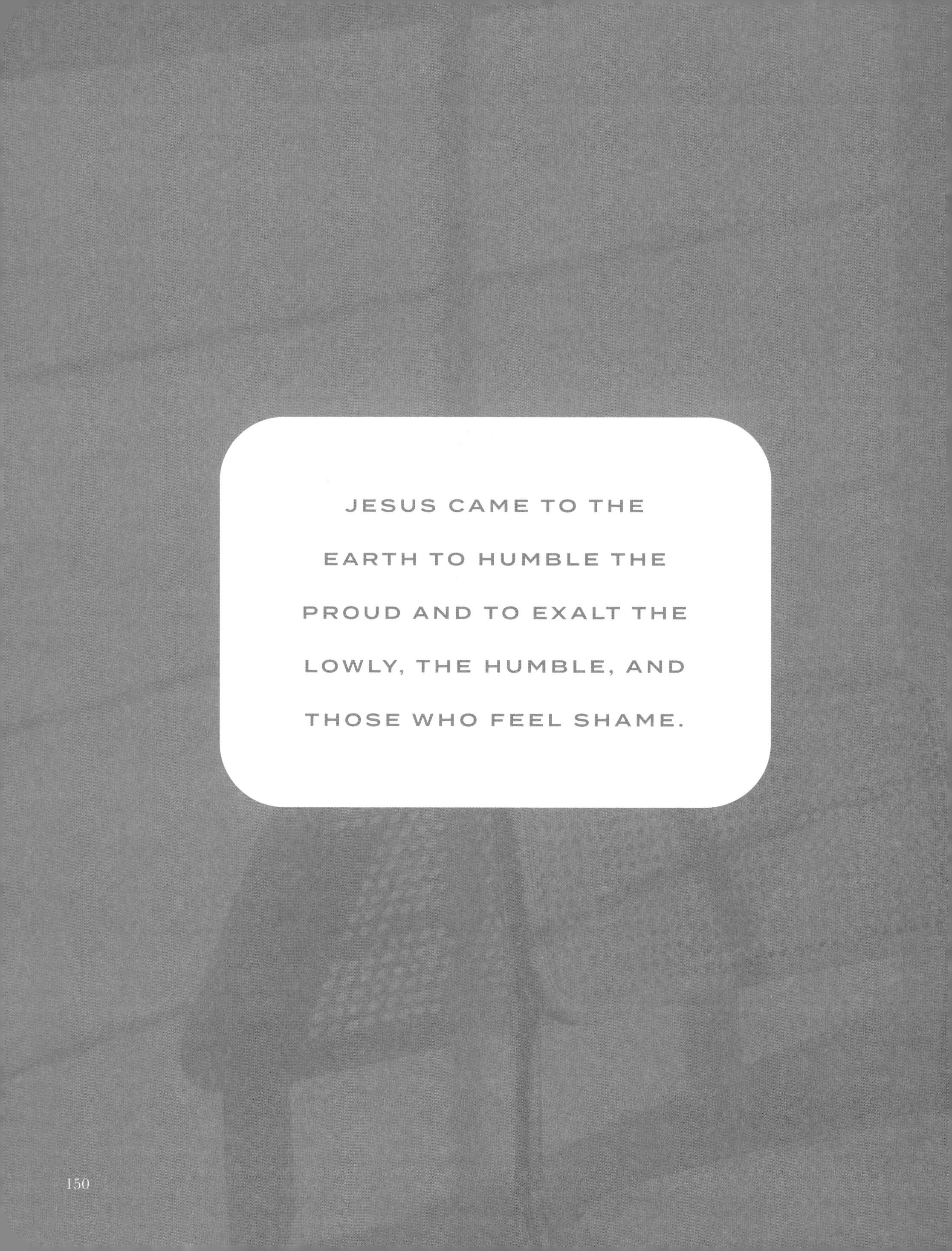

JESUS CAME TO THE EARTH TO HUMBLE THE PROUD AND TO EXALT THE LOWLY, THE HUMBLE, AND THOSE WHO FEEL SHAME.

MARK IT UP

Old Testament Passage

We will begin our week with a study of 1 Samuel 2:1–10 and see how these verses show us God's heart for the humble and lowly. Read the passage multiple times and annotate, or mark up, the text as you read. For tips and examples on annotating, see page 196–207.

1. Highlight any words or phrases that point to Christ.

2. Make note of any attributes of God seen in the text.

3. Who are the two groups of people discussed in the passage? Circle words that describe them.

4. Underline any instances of irony you see in the passage (i.e., anywhere in which the events of Scripture happen contrary to how you might expect).

1 SAMUEL 2:1–10

1 Hannah prayed:

My heart rejoices in the LORD; my horn is lifted up by
the LORD. My mouth boasts over my enemies, because
I rejoice in your salvation. 2 There is no one holy like
the LORD. There is no one besides you! And there is no
rock like our God. 3 Do not boast so proudly, or let
arrogant words come out of your mouth, for the LORD is
a God of knowledge, and actions are weighed by him.
4 The bows of the warriors are broken, but the feeble
are clothed with strength. 5 Those who are full hire
themselves out for food, but those who are starving
hunger no more. The woman who is childless gives birth
to seven, but the woman with many sons pines away.

6 The Lord brings death and gives life; he sends some
down to Sheol, and he raises others up. 7 The Lord brings
poverty and gives wealth; he humbles and he exalts.
8 He raises the poor from the dust and lifts the needy
from the trash heap. He seats them with noblemen and
gives them a throne of honor. For the foundations of
the earth are the Lord's; he has set the world on them.
9 He guards the steps of his faithful ones, but the wicked
perish in darkness, for a person does not prevail by
his own strength. 10 Those who oppose the Lord will be
shattered;, he will thunder in the heavens against them.
The Lord will judge the ends of the earth. He will give
power to his king; he will lift up the horn of his anointed.

Go Deeper

1 Read 1 Samuel 1:1–2:10.

Throughout this study, we have mostly focused on big events, important leaders, or the nation of Israel as a whole, but this week's reading will focus on Hannah—an ordinary but devout Israelite woman. Hannah's situation is not unfamiliar to us. Like many other women we meet in the Old Testament, she is childless.

2 In your own words, describe how you think Hannah felt as a childless woman.

In ancient Israel where Hannah lives, children are a lifeline for women. There are very few opportunities for women to have any financial independence, especially if they are widowed. Hannah likely feels great insecurity about her future livelihood.

In addition, not having children brings about great social shame for women. Hannah no doubt feels like an outcast in many ways, but we are told explicitly that her husband's other wife—who is able to have children—taunts and ridicules her for her barrenness. Hannah likely feels great shame, great longing, and great sorrow.

In her sadness, Hannah prays at the house of the Lord (1 Samuel 1:10–11), pleading with God for a child. This prayer shows us her longing, but it also shows us her knowledge of and trust in God. She knows that He hears her prayers. She knows He sees her pain, and she believes He has the power to give her a child.

Like many of us are tempted to do, she makes a vow to God in her desperation. She promises that she will give her child back to Him if He grants her request. But unlike most people in this situation, we see that she follows through on her vow (1 Samuel 1:28)—and more than that, she experiences relief from her sorrow *before* God even gives her a child (1 Samuel 1:18).

Hannah does not find satisfaction in her husband, though he does love her. She does not find it in her circumstances, as nothing has changed yet. Instead, Hannah's relief and satisfaction come from praying to God. She knows His character and trusts His goodness, even without a change in her earthly circumstances.

3 Read 1 Samuel 1:17–18 and 1:26–28 again. What do these verses tell us about Hannah's character?

Eventually, the Lord does fulfill Hannah's request for a son. And when He does so, Hannah not only keeps her vow—she also praises the Lord. Only her knowledge of God, His character, and His heart for her could produce the beautiful prayer and prophecy we read in 1 Samuel 2.

4 What does Hannah's prayer (1 Samuel 2:1–10) reveal about the character of God?

Hannah's prayer reveals much about the character and heart of God. She begins by acknowledging His sovereignty and power and then that He can humble whom He wills and exalt whom He wills (1 Samuel 2:7). This truth makes the next verse all the more meaningful for people like Hannah. In His perfect power and authority, He chooses to exalt the poor, needy, and humble, and He brings down the proud, the wicked, and those who try to succeed by their own strength and power.

Hannah experiences this firsthand, as God sees her in her affliction, need, and humility and chooses her to bear the prophet who would anoint and advise Israel's great King David (1 Samuel 16:13). God also uses Hannah to proclaim God's deliverance through Jesus—the Messiah, Israel's true King, who would later come to bring shame to the powerful and exalt the humble (1 Samuel 2:10).

GOD — THE ALL-POWERFUL CREATOR AND RULER OF ALL THINGS — HUMBLED HIMSELF.

MARK IT UP

New Testament Passage

After studying the prayer of Hannah over the past two days, we will now move to the New Testament to read a similar song of praise—this time, coming from the mouth of Mary, the mother of Jesus. Read Luke 1:46–55 multiple times and annotate, or mark up, the text as you read. For tips and examples on annotating, see page 196–207.

1. Highlight any words or phrases that point to Christ.

2. Make note of any attributes of God seen in the text.

3. Circle all of the actions that Mary proclaims God has done.

4. Underline any instances of irony you see in this passage as well (i.e., anywhere in which the events of Scripture happen contrary to how you might expect).

5. Look back at 1 Samuel 2:1–10. Make note of any parallel words, phrases, or ideas (i.e., words, phrases, or ideas that share the same or a similar construction).

LUKE 1:46–55

46 And Mary said:

My soul magnifies the Lord, 47 and my spirit rejoices in
God my Savior, 48 because he has looked with favor on
the humble condition of his servant. Surely, from now
on all generations will call me blessed, 49 because the
Mighty One has done great things for me, and his name
is holy. 50 His mercy is from generation to generation

on those who fear him. 51 He has done a mighty deed
with his arm; he has scattered the proud because
of the thoughts of their hearts; 52 he has toppled
the mighty from their thrones and exalted the lowly.
53 He has satisfied the hungry with good things and
sent the rich away empty. 54 He has helped his servant
Israel, remembering his mercy 55 to Abraham and his
descendants forever, just as he spoke to our ancestors.

Make the Christ Connection

1 Read 1 Samuel 2:1–10 and Luke 1:26–55.

Like Hannah, Mary is just an ordinary Jewish girl—only Mary is not in Hannah's predicament of sorrow. She has her entire life ahead of her—she is betrothed to a young man from her town and is set up for success. Then, she receives a message from an angel who tells her that her life is about to change.

2 As a young, unmarried girl, how would you expect Mary to respond to the angel's message?

Most young, unmarried girls would probably want to run in the other direction. The shame and social stigma that often accompany a teenage pregnancy today would only be magnified in Mary's day. She has every reason to fear this reality, as it would likely result in being shunned by her friends and family. And since she is betrothed, it has the possibility of ending in death (Deuteronomy 22:20–24).

But if Mary is concerned with any of this, she does not show it. Instead, she submits herself to the will of God and simply says, "I am the Lord's servant" (Luke 1:38). We are told that she has found favor with God (Luke 1:30), and based on her response, we can conclude that she knows His heart for His people. Only genuine trust would yield such a response.

3 How does Mary's situation compare or contrast to Hannah's?

Like Hannah, Mary is childless. But where Hannah's absence of pregnancy caused her social shame and financial insecurity, the presence of a pregnancy in Mary's life would have these same effects. However, even in the face of shame and hardship, both women submit themselves to God and His will, knowing that He cares for them.

The connection between these two women and their stories is made explicit through their parallel words of prayer and praise. They begin with praise and rejoicing in their salvation (1 Samuel 2:1, Luke 1:46–47), and both focus on the intentions of God to exalt the humble and bring down the proud (1 Samuel 2:3, 7–8, 10; Luke 1:51–53).

However, perhaps more than these connections, the words of both women point beyond themselves and their current situations to God's redemption through Christ.

4 Read Philippians 2:5–11. How do Hannah and Mary's words point us to God's purposes through Christ?

It is in Jesus that we see the lowly, humble, and ashamed being exalted and the proud and wicked brought down. But before this reversal could happen, another one was necessary.

God—the all-powerful Creator and Ruler of all things—humbled Himself. By coming to earth in human flesh, Jesus became the lowly, the needy, and the poor (2 Corinthians 8:9). Then, He also took on the sin and shame of humanity when He hung on the cross and died.

Death by crucifixion was one of the most physically excruciating and psychologically humiliating forms of capital punishment. It was engineered to bring its victims as much humiliation, shame, and pain as possible.

But as we know, that was not the end. Three days after His death, Jesus arose from the grave and was exalted again in His resurrection and ascension to heaven, where he sits at the right hand of God. All of this so that we—the lowly, sinful, shameful human beings who put our trust in Him—can be exalted with Him while His enemies—the proud and wicked who reject Him—will be put to shame. It is this reversal, this great act of compassion and redemption, to which the words of Hannah and Mary point us.

Live it Out

1 Read 1 Samuel 2:1–10 and Luke 1:46–55.

Through both Hannah's prayer and Mary's song—and the lives of these two women—we learn about the character of God. Specifically, we see His heart for those who are considered lowly, humble, needy, poor, and shameful. We learn how Hannah and Mary's words point to Christ's great endurance of humiliation—taking on human flesh and being crucified—and His exaltation—His resurrection and ascension. These events make a way for lowly humans to be exalted with Christ if they put their faith in Him.

Not only do the words in this week's passages teach us about God's character, but they also compel us to pursue a deeper knowledge of God. The lives of Hannah and Mary reveal the importance of knowing the character of God when we face difficult situations. Their stories ought to compel us to continuously seek to grow in our knowledge and love of God through Scripture so that we may find true satisfaction in Him.

REFLECT ON THE WORDS OF THESE PRAYERS AS YOU ANSWER THE FOLLOWING QUESTIONS.

2 In what ways do you or have you experienced shame in your life?

3 What aspects of God's character encourage you in your current circumstances?

4 Hannah and Mary found joy through placing their hope and their satisfaction in God. How can you practically find satisfaction in Christ rather than in your possessions or circumstances?

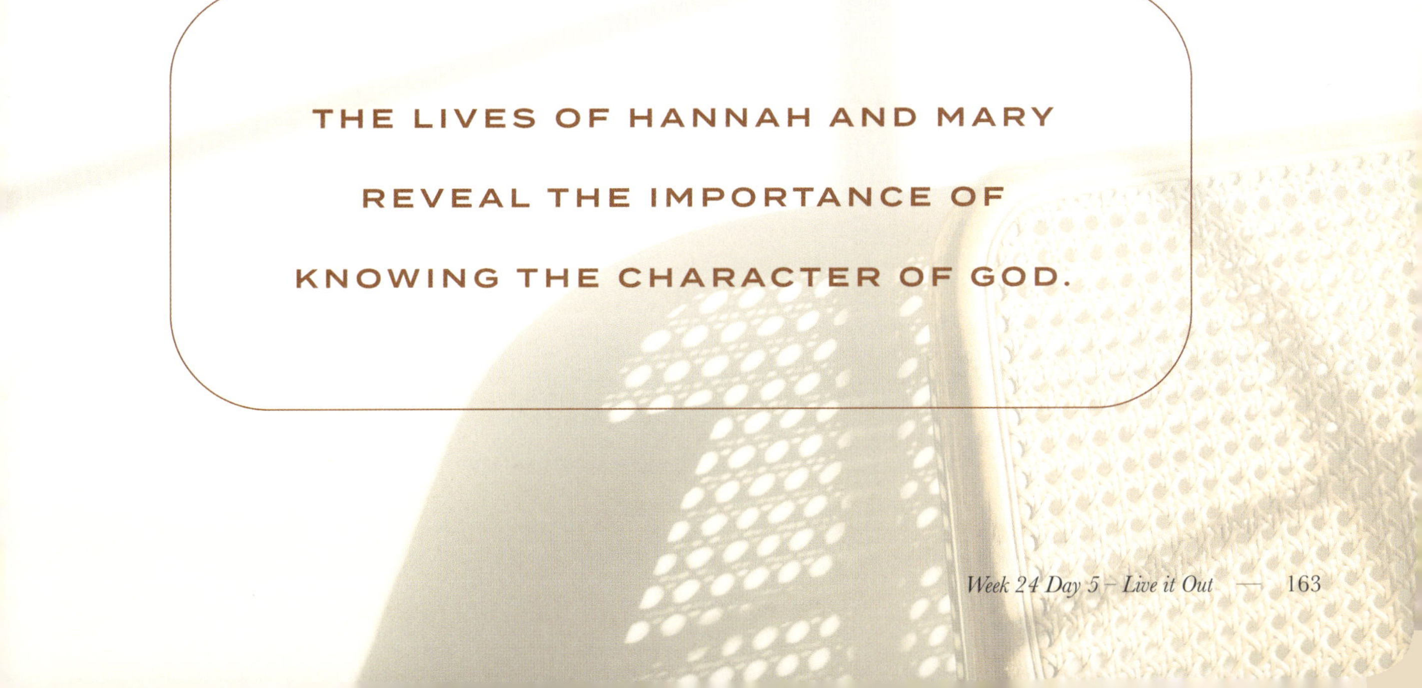

THE LIVES OF HANNAH AND MARY REVEAL THE IMPORTANCE OF KNOWING THE CHARACTER OF GOD.

Introduction

WEEK TWENTY-FIVE

This week, you will study the account of David and Goliath in 1 Samuel 17:41–50, as well as Paul's encouragement to the Corinthian church in 1 Corinthians 1:26–31. You will learn that God's wisdom far surpasses human wisdom, for only God would choose to have His only Son die for the sins of guilty people. In doing so, you will be encouraged to trust less in your own wisdom and more in God's limitless understanding.

GOD'S WISDOM

FAR SURPASSES

HUMAN WISDOM.

MARK IT UP

Old Testament Passage

Today, we will begin studying 1 Samuel 17:41–50, which describes the famous battle between the shepherd boy David and the Philistine warrior Goliath. This narrative teaches us that God's wisdom is greater than human wisdom, pointing toward the day when the death of God's Son would accomplish salvation for God's people. Read the passage multiple times and annotate, or mark up, the text as you read. For tips and examples on annotating, see page 196–207.

1. Highlight any words or phrases that point to Christ.

2. Make note of any attributes of God seen in the text.

3. Circle the weapons that Goliath used.

4. Now, circle the weapons that David used. What do you think is significant about the difference between these two weapons?

5. Underline any references to God or the Lord between verses 45–47. How does this repetition help us understand where David's confidence lies?

41 The Philistine came closer and closer to David, with the
shield-bearer in front of him. 42 When the Philistine looked
and saw David, he despised him because he was just a youth,
healthy and handsome. 43 He said to David, "Am I a dog that
you come against me with sticks?" Then he cursed David
by his gods. 44 "Come here," the Philistine called to David,
"and I'll give your flesh to the birds of the sky and the wild
beasts!" 45 David said to the Philistine, "You come against
me with a sword, spear, and javelin, but I come against you
in the name of the LORD of Armies, the God of the ranks of
Israel — you have defied him. 46 Today, the LORD will hand you
over to me. Today, I'll strike you down, remove your head,

and give the corpses of the Philistine camp to the birds of the
sky and the wild creatures of the earth. Then all the world
will know that Israel has a God, 47 and this whole assembly
will know that it is not by sword or by spear that the Lord
saves, for the battle is the Lord's. He will hand you over to us."
48 When the Philistine started forward to attack him, David
ran quickly to the battle line to meet the Philistine. 49 David
put his hand in the bag, took out a stone, slung it, and hit the
Philistine on his forehead. The stone sank into his forehead,
and he fell facedown to the ground. 50 David defeated the
Philistine with a sling and a stone. David overpowered
the Philistine and killed him without having a sword.

Go Deeper

1 Read 1 Samuel 17:41–50.

The account of David and Goliath is one of the most famous in Scripture. While the Israelites cower in fear under Goliath's threats, David, a mere shepherd boy, rises in courage to fight the Philistine champion—not in his own strength but in the Lord's. Through this narrative of David's victory in 1 Samuel 17, we see a common theme that is repeated throughout Scripture—God's wisdom is far greater than man's. He will use the weak to showcase His strength.

2 Read 1 Samuel 17:1–32. How does this passage describe Goliath?

First Samuel 17 provides many details about Goliath, his armor, and his taunts against the Israelites. The Philistines were not only strong; they were well-defended—a threat Israel could have avoided all together if they had obeyed the Lord's instruction.

Upon Israel's entrance into the Promised Land, God had commanded them to drive out the natives who were settled there and take the land as their own (Deuteronomy 20:16–18). However, the Israelites failed to do so (Joshua 13:1–3) and instead lived in continuous conflict with the Philistines and the other Canaanite nations left in the Promised Land.

3 Read Judges 1:18–19. According to these verses, why did the Israelites fear the people of the plain? Now, think back to the description of Goliath in 1 Samuel 17:4–7. Why do you think the Israelites feared him?

The author of 1 Samuel takes great care to describe Goliath's bronze helmet, coat of armor, and even the iron point upon his spear. Clearly, the Philistines are strong and outfitted with the most advanced weaponry of the day. The Israelites feel outmatched in their battle against Goliath and his army.

Israel should remember God's faithfulness to bring them out of Egypt, part the Red Sea, provide manna in the wilderness, and bring them safely to the Promised Land. But they look at the strength of their enemies instead of the strength of God. Their actions are ultimately driven by worldly wisdom—which urges them to flee a strong enemy—rather than God's wisdom, which should give them confidence in God's deliverance.

4 Read 1 Samuel 17:33–37. What gives David confidence that the Lord will fight on his behalf?

In comparison to the might and advancement of Goliath, David, the youngest of eight brothers, seems a laughable opponent. David neither possesses weapons made of iron nor extensive military experience. His training has been in the pasture; his experience consists of protecting his sheep.

Conventional wisdom would likely call David naive, perhaps even foolish. But David has witnessed God's everyday faithfulness as he has fought bears and lions, and this faithfulness gives David confidence that God will be faithful to him once again.

5 Finally, read 1 Samuel 17:38–50.

God proves faithful to the faith-filled shepherd boy. Goliath is struck down—not by military prowess—but by a boy with a few stones and a sling because David trusts that God is much bigger than the enemy—infinite in power, strength, resources, and wisdom.

Isaiah 40:28 reminds us that the Lord is the everlasting God. He never becomes faint or weary; there is no limit to His understanding. Hundreds of years later, God would again defy conventional wisdom by clothing Himself in human flesh to rescue His people once and for all.

Indeed, God's wisdom is far greater than our own.

6 Pray that God would increase your faith in Him so that you may have the courage to trust in His wisdom rather than your own.

conventional wisdom: A generally accepted belief or opinion.

MARK IT UP

New Testament Passage

Yesterday, by looking at the Old Testament story of David and Goliath, we learned how God's strength and wisdom is always greater than our own. Today, we will see that truth on display again as we turn to Paul's words in the New Testament. Read 1 Corinthians 1:26–31 multiple times and annotate, or mark up, the text as you read. For tips and examples on annotating, see page 196–207.

1 Highlight any words or phrases that point to Christ.

2 Make note of any attributes of God seen in the text.

3 Circle what the text says that God has chosen.

4 Draw a box around any time these verses say "in the world." How do these annotations help you distinguish between God's wisdom and earthly wisdom?

5 Underline how Jesus became wisdom from God for us in verse 30.

1 CORINTHIANS 1:26–31

26 Brothers and sisters, consider your calling: Not many
were wise from a human perspective, not many powerful,
not many of noble birth. 27 Instead, God has chosen what
is foolish in the world to shame the wise, and God has
chosen what is weak in the world to shame the strong.
28 God has chosen what is insignificant and despised in the
world — what is viewed as nothing — to bring to nothing
what is viewed as something, 29 so that no one may boast in
his presence. 30 It is from him that you are in Christ Jesus,
who became wisdom from God for us — our righteousness,
sanctification, and redemption — 31 in order that, as it is
written: Let the one who boasts, boast in the Lord.

Make the Christ Connection

1 Read 1 Samuel 17:41–50 and 1 Corinthians 1:11–31.

Libraries hold hundreds or thousands of books with words and pages that contain more knowledge than one human can grasp. But even greater than all the words and pages written within every book throughout human history is the knowledge of God. In fact, God's knowledge is so vast that no amount of literature could ever contain it.

2 First Corinthians 1:11–31 is a passage that discusses the wisdom of God. How would you summarize this passage in a sentence or two?

When writing to the church in Corinth, Paul reminds them that God's wisdom is not only vast but that it is fundamentally different from human wisdom. God's wisdom does not operate within human bounds—rather, it is limitless and infinite.

David understood God's infinite capabilities when he stepped forward to battle Goliath with no coat of armor or conventional military weapon (1 Samuel 17:49). David knew that God's strength surpassed that of the Philistine's (1 Samuel 17:45). Indeed, God's wisdom accomplished a victory that likely seemed impossible to Israel's fearful army.

3 Once again, read 1 Corinthians 1:11–17. Why is Paul writing to the Corinthians about the difference between earthly wisdom and godly wisdom?

In this passage, the Corinthians are experiencing division amongst each other. They are using earthly wisdom to exalt themselves—and this pride is fracturing the local church. Therefore, Paul reminds them of their foundation. Though they are not wise by the world's standards, God has chosen them despite their weakness to be adopted as sons and daughters of God by grace through faith in Christ. Even in their own story, God proves strong through their weakness. Their own salvation is an example of God's wisdom defying earthly wisdom.

4 Read Proverbs 28:26. What is the result of those who trust not in their own ways but in God's wisdom?

Just as God delivered David from the might of Goliath, just as He delivered the Israelites from Egyptian oppression, just as He delivered Jonah from the belly of the fish, just as He delivered Daniel from the lion's den—God will also deliver those who trust in God's wisdom. And though His wisdom may not produce the outcomes we desire or expect, we can trust that God's wisdom and His capabilities far surpass our own.

And this is proven in Christ. In 1 Corinthians 1:22–24, Paul says that Christ crucified is "a stumbling block to the Jews and foolishness to the Gentiles." The Jews believe a cross is a symbol of cursing, and the Gentiles cannot fathom a religion in which the Savior dies a criminal's death on the cross. Both the Jewish and the Gentile perspectives represent the world's wisdom—unable to comprehend the magnitude of God's love for His people.

Jesus is the true and better David. In God's wisdom, He chose to lower Himself to the weakness of mankind and die a criminal's death to conquer the Goliath called sin. Only in God's wisdom would Christ's greatest weapon over the enemy be Himself. Only in God's wisdom could one perfect man pay the cost of sin for all of God's people.

Jesus is not just a part of God's perfectly wise story of redemption. Jesus is God's wisdom personified, for Jesus is God Himself.

Live it Out

1 Read 1 Samuel 17:41–50 and 1 Corinthians 1:26–31.

Can you imagine what the Israelite army was thinking as David stepped up to battle Goliath? They likely thought he was foolish to believe he could take on such a fearsome warrior. And yet, God did the impossible through David's faith. Conventional wisdom was proven foolish, and David, trusting in his Lord, was proven wise. God's wisdom often turns human expectations upside down.

While the world says more and better is best, Christ demonstrated that God's power is made perfect in weakness, for the King of kings surrendered Himself to a shameful death on the cross. Jesus became weak, in the form of man—a man who faced brutality and mockery—so that God's strength could be proven through His resurrection. Yes, Jesus died. But He rose from the grave in power, defeating sin's chokehold on humanity. Human wisdom would never choose the cross, but God's wisdom saw beyond the grave to a glorious victory.

When we live our lives fixated on the gospel, we are able to view weakness differently than the world does. When we swell with pride, we can remind ourselves of our salvation in Christ—that we are weak sinners, cleansed from our sin and adopted by God, recipients of a gift we could never earn. Yet when we feel weak, we do not have to sit in shame, for from David's story—and Jesus's example—we learn that God's power is made perfect in weakness (2 Corinthians 12:9). When we are weak, we look to Christ as our strength. Our faith is anchored in God's ability and not our own.

REFLECT ON THIS WEEK'S VERSES AS YOU ANSWER THE FOLLOWING QUESTIONS.

2 How can you grow in your ability to discern between God's wisdom and the world's wisdom?

3 Reflect upon a time when your own strength or ability failed you. Did your weakness teach you to rely on God's strength?

4 Write out a prayer, thanking Jesus for becoming weak and experiencing the brutality of the cross so that God's strength would be proven through His resurrection.

HUMAN WISDOM WOULD NEVER CHOOSE THE CROSS, BUT GOD'S WISDOM SAW BEYOND THE GRAVE TO A GLORIOUS VICTORY.

Introduction

WEEK TWENTY-SIX

This week, we will look at one of the most pivotal moments in the Bible: when God makes a covenant with King David (2 Samuel 7:12–16). We will see how the promise of this covenant sustains the nation of Israel through dark times and how Jesus ultimately fulfills this covenant (Luke 1:32–33). In response, we will gain a fresh appreciation for Jesus's role as our perfect and eternal King and be comforted by the reminder that He currently reigns from His throne.

MARK IT UP

Old Testament Passage

We will start this week by studying the covenant God made with King David, which is found in 2 Samuel 7:12–16. Read the passage two or three times and annotate, or mark up, the text as you read. For tips and examples on annotating, see page 196–207.

1. Highlight any words or phrases that point to Christ.
2. Make note of any attributes of God seen in the text.
3. Circle repeated words found in this promise
4. Underline words that express the duration of this kingdom.
5. How does God describe His relationship to the king in verse 14?

2 SAMUEL 7:12–16

12 When your time comes and you rest with your ancestors,
I will raise up after you your descendant, who will come from
your body, and I will establish his kingdom. 13 He is the one who
will build a house for my name, and I will establish the throne
of his kingdom forever. 14 I will be his father, and he will be my
son. When he does wrong, I will discipline him with a rod of
men and blows from mortals. 15 But my faithful love will never
leave him as it did when I removed it from Saul, whom I removed
from before you. 16 Your house and kingdom will endure before
me forever, and your throne will be established forever.

Go Deeper

1 Read 2 Samuel 7:1–17.

The book of 1 Samuel records an important transition for the people of Israel: the establishment of a monarchy. Up to this point in their life as a nation, Israel has not been ruled by a king, but there have been indications that one day, they would be. God told Abraham that kings would come from him (Genesis 17:6). A future ruler was promised to Judah (Genesis 49:8–12). Moses gave instructions on how a future king must behave (Deuteronomy 17:14–20), and the dark days of the judges are referred to as a period when no king ruled over Israel (Judges 17:6, 18:1, 19:1, 21:25).

God chose Saul to be the first king of Israel, and his reign started off well enough. But when Saul rejected God by sinning against Him, God announced through the prophet Samuel that He had rejected Saul as king (1 Samuel 15:26). God also had Samuel anoint David—"a man after [God's] own heart" (1 Samuel 13:14)—to be the next king of Israel (1 Samuel 16). Much of the rest of 1 Samuel tells of how David spent years as a fugitive, fleeing from the murderous King Saul.

2 Read 1 Samuel 24:1–7. In these verses, Saul goes into a cave, not knowing it is where David and his men are hiding, to relieve himself. How does David demonstrate his faith in God in this scene?

Several chapters later, when we turn to the book of 2 Samuel, we finally see David's reign over Israel, and there are some notable transitions in this book as well. In chapter 5, David captures Jerusalem and makes it Israel's capital. And in chapter 6, he brings the ark of the covenant—which represents God's presence—to Jerusalem. Then, in chapter 7, David expresses a desire to build a permanent temple to house the ark.

God's response to David is a pivotal moment in the Bible. It is not David who will build a house for God; rather, God will build a house for David. In other words, a temple (i.e., a "house") *will* be built by David's son, referring to Solomon. But God will build David a dynasty (i.e., a "house"). Unlike Saul's dynasty, which died with him, David's dynasty will never end. It will be established forever.

3 How does David respond to God's promise in 2 Samuel 7:18–29?

God's words to David here in 2 Samuel reverberate throughout the Bible. They are reflected in Psalms 89 and 132. Psalm 2:7 meditates on the father-son relationship that God has with Israel's Davidic king, saying, "You [the king] are my Son; today I have become your Father." And even when the kingdom declined and God's people went into exile, prophets like Isaiah clung to God's promise to David for hope, writing in Isaiah 9:6–7, "For a child will be born for us, a son will be given to us . . . He will reign on the throne of David and over his kingdom . . ."

4 Read Jeremiah 23:1–6. What role does God's promise to David play in this passage? How is it used to comfort God's people?

For the Israelites, God's promise to David shone like a light in the darkness. It gave them assurance that the dark days of the exile would one day be over and that a righteous King was coming.

anoint: Throughout the Old Testament, various objects and people were anointed with oil (representing God's Spirit), setting them apart for service to God. This included kings. Psalm 2:2 uses the Hebrew term *messiah* ("anointed one") to describe Israel's king. In the gospels, Jesus is anointed with the Spirit (Luke 3:22), and the term *Messiah*—along with its Greek equivalent, *Christ*—is applied to Him.

MARK IT UP

New Testament Passage

Yesterday, we studied the covenant God made with King David in 2 Samuel 7. Today, we will turn to the Gospel of Luke to see how Jesus perfectly and eternally fulfills that covenant. Read Luke 1:32–33 two or three times and annotate, or mark up, the text as you read. For tips and examples on annotating, see page 196–207.

1. Highlight any words or phrases that point to Christ.
2. Make note of any attributes of God seen in the text.
3. Circle any references you see to God's promise to David.
4. What kind of king is being described here?
5. What kind of kingdom is being described?

LUKE 1:32–33

32 He will be great and will be called the Son of the
Most High, and the Lord God will give him the throne
of his father David. 33 He will reign over the house of
Jacob forever, and his kingdom will have no end.

Make the Christ Connection

1 Read 2 Samuel 7:12–16 and Luke 1:26–38.

In His covenant with David, God promised that any kings from his line who disobeyed Him would be punished (2 Samuel 7:12–16, Psalm 89:30–37). In the following centuries, David's dynasty tragically fell into increasing wickedness, and true to His promise, God judged them by sending the Babylonians to attack Jerusalem, burn the temple, and take its population into exile.

The Exile was a dark moment in Israel's history. But God had also promised that David's line would last forever, and this promise provided a glimmer of hope in the darkness. We see this glimmer at the very end of 2 Kings, when the Davidic king Jehoiachin is shown kindness while in exile (2 Kings 25:27–30). We see it in 1 Chronicles 3:17–24, which records David's line being preserved through the Exile, and in Isaiah 11:1–2, which speaks of a future Davidic king on whom the Spirit will rest. And we see this glimmer of hope reach a crescendo when the angel Gabriel approaches a young virgin named Mary and tells her she will conceive and give birth to a son.

2 How do you think Mary felt when she heard the news that she—a virgin—would conceive and that her child would sit on David's throne?

Gabriel lets Mary know in no uncertain terms that her child—Jesus—will be the long-awaited King who will fulfill God's promises to David. He is the child of whom Isaiah spoke: on whose shoulders the government would rest and who would reign over and establish David's kingdom "with justice and righteousness from now on and forever" (Isaiah 9:6–7).

Jesus's connection to David is further emphasized in Luke 3:21–22. After Jesus is baptized, the Holy Spirit descends on Him, just as Isaiah 11:1–2 prophesied. A voice from heaven declares, "You are my beloved Son; with you I am well-pleased"—words taken from Psalm 2:7, which were originally spoken to Israel's Davidic king. And this scene is followed by a genealogy that shows Jesus's descent from David and thus His right to sit on David's throne. Jesus is the Son of God, the true King who has come to sit on David's throne and never leave it.

3 Compare Psalm 89:30–32 with what is said about Jesus in 2 Corinthians 5:21 and Hebrews 4:15. In what way is Jesus very different from the other kings from David's line?

Many wicked kings ruled from David's throne. And even the good ones were flawed. But in contrast to these previous kings, Jesus is without sin. And that means He indeed rules forever with perfect justice and perfect righteousness, just as Isaiah prophesied in Isaiah 9:7.

This King—Jesus—died, was buried, rose again, and ascended into heaven, where He now sits at the right hand of the Father. And He has promised to come back for us! Like the Israelites in the Old Testament, we wait for the King to arrive—but this time, we are waiting for Him to arrive for a second, final time. When He returns, He will fully establish His kingdom here on the earth, and He will banish sin and death forever. Until then, we wait with expectation, and we invite others to become part of His kingdom (Matthew 28:18–20).

4 Spend time praising God for sending Jesus to be a righteous and just ruler.

Live it Out

1 Read 2 Samuel 7:12–16 and Luke 1:32–33.

A King who never sins, who always does what is right, who rules justly and shows no favoritism.

Simply to read of such a King can make our hearts ache. Even the best rulers of our world fall short of this and, at the end of the day, pass away. And all too often, rulers tragically use their positions of power to benefit themselves at the expense of others.

Jesus is the King our hearts ache for. And though He did die, He rose from the grave and will never die again. It is through His death and resurrection that we can become citizens of His kingdom.

For now, our hearts still ache. We ache for Jesus to return and bring His kingdom in its fullness, a kingdom in which sin, sickness, tears, and even death will be forever eradicated (Revelation 21:1–4). Until that day, we remember His words, "I am coming soon," and pray in response, "Amen! Come, Lord Jesus!" (Revelation 22:20).

REFLECT ON THIS WEEK'S VERSES AS YOU ANSWER THE FOLLOWING QUESTIONS.

2 What are some ways in which life is difficult for you right now? How does the assurance of Jesus's return speak to those difficulties and inform how you respond to them?

3 According to Matthew 28:18–20, how can we work to spread Jesus's kingdom here on earth right now?

4 Meditate on Colossians 1:13–14 and give God thanks for bringing you into the kingdom of His Son.

JESUS IS THE KING OUR HEARTS ACHE FOR.

Tracing the Davidic Covenant Through the Prophets

As the southern kingdom of Judah—where David's throne was located—slid into further sin and was exiled to Babylon, it might have seemed as though many of God's promises to Israel had failed. But the prophets spoke of a glorious future for God's people, and key to that future was the arrival of a King who would sit on David's throne forever, just as God had promised. Below are some examples of how the prophets appealed to the Davidic covenant for this future hope.

Note: You will notice mention of Jesse in the first example verse. Jesse is David's father.

ISAIAH 11:1–2

Then a shoot will grow from the stump of Jesse, and a branch from his roots will bear fruit. The Spirit of the LORD will rest on him—a Spirit of wisdom and understanding, a Spirit of counsel and strength, a Spirit of knowledge and of the fear of the LORD.

JEREMIAH 23:5

"Look, the days are coming"—this is the LORD's declaration—"when I will raise up a Righteous Branch for David. He will reign wisely as king and administer justice and righteousness in the land."

JEREMIAH 33:17

For this is what the Lord says: David will never fail to have a man sitting on the throne of the house of Israel.

EZEKIEL 34:23

I will establish over them one shepherd, my servant David, and he will shepherd them. He will tend them himself and will be their shepherd.

HOSEA 3:5

Afterward, the people of Israel will return and seek the Lord their God and David their king. They will come with awe to the Lord and to his goodness in the last days.

AMOS 9:11

In that day I will restore the fallen shelter of David: I will repair its gaps, restore its ruins, and rebuild it as in the days of old.

Volume 2 Conclusion

Congratulations! If you have reached this page, that means you have made it through the second of four volumes in the *Christ in All of Scripture* study set. In other words, you have now spent half a year discovering how we can see Christ on every page of God's Word!

Over the past twenty-six weeks, you have read, annotated, and considered many passages from across the Old and New Testaments. And in doing so, you have begun to see how all of Scripture—even the most unexpected and hard-to-understand passages—points us to Jesus Christ.

We covered a lot of ground in this volume alone. From God's presence filling the tabernacle to the role of the prophets, from His provision in the lives of Ruth and Naomi to His everlasting covenant with King David—we have seen how each and every detail finds its ultimate fulfillment in Jesus Christ. This truth should lead our hearts to awe and wonder as we worship our great Savior and give Him thanks for His glorious plan of redemption.

Yet we also must recognize that the story of Scripture does not end here. As the pages of the Bible continue to unfold, there are many more exciting Christ connections to be made! So, we invite you to continue your study with us in *Christ in All of Scripture | Volume 3*, which covers Old Testament passages from the rebuilding of God's temple after the Exile (Ezra 3) to Isaiah's prophecy of the person and work of Jesus Christ (Isaiah 52, 53). As we study these passages, we will continue to be pointed—in a myriad of ways—to Christ and His work on our behalf.

As we continue to study God's Word, may we continually grow in our love for Him. May we rejoice in His glorious plan of redemption, which is on display from the first pages of Genesis to the final chapters of Revelation. And may we ultimately worship Christ for all He has done on our behalf. He is the main character of the story. And so, let us continue to commit ourselves to seeing His fingerprints on every page.

You can find Christ in All of Scripture | Volume 3 *— along with all subsequent volumes and many more resources to equip you in your study of God's Word — at www.thedailygraceco.com.*

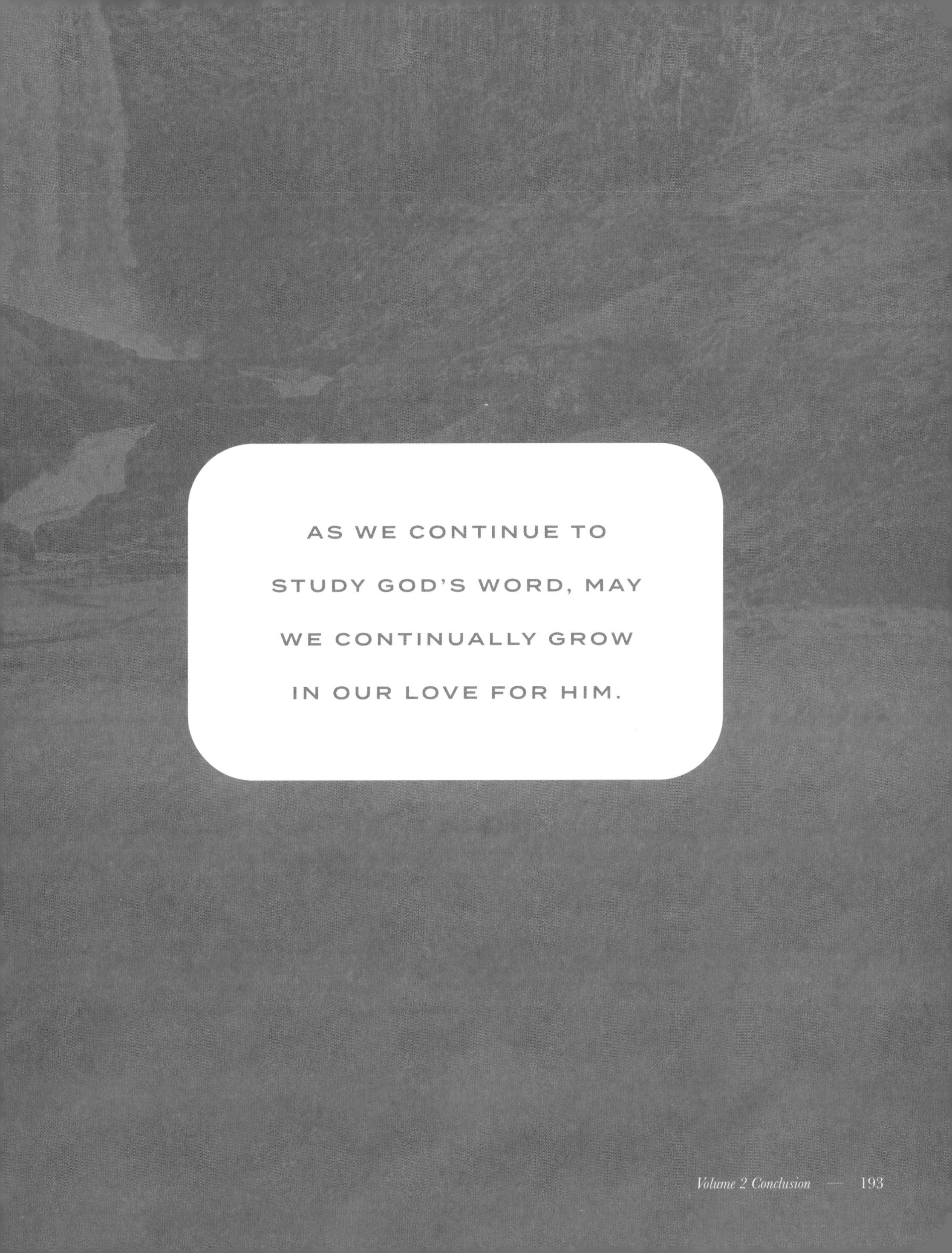

AS WE CONTINUE TO STUDY GOD'S WORD, MAY WE CONTINUALLY GROW IN OUR LOVE FOR HIM.

APPENDIX

The content in this Appendix is adapted from Week 1: Prep Week from the first volume of this study. To access the full Prep Week content—complete with more examples and illustrations—check out *Christ in All of Scripture | Volume 1*, available at www.thedailygraceco.com, or scan the QR code below.

How to See Christ in All of Scripture

The study you hold in your hands centers on how we can find Christ in all of Scripture. But practically, how can we do so? The following chart describes seven elements you can look for in each passage—along with examples from the story of Noah in Genesis 6–9—that will point you in the right direction as you journey through Scripture. You may not find each of these elements in every passage you study, but often, one or more will be present, pointing you to Jesus Christ—even in the most unexpected places.

WHAT TO LOOK FOR	EXAMPLE (FROM GENESIS 6–9)
Roles: Positions seen throughout Scripture that are filled perfectly by Christ	There are many roles in the Old Testament that find their fulfillment in Christ. We can see this specifically in the roles of prophets, priests, and kings—three roles which Jesus perfectly fulfilled through His life, death, resurrection, and ascension into heaven. But there are more than just these. For example, Noah plays the role of a leader in Genesis 6–9 as he leads his family to salvation through the ark, just as Christ leads His people to salvation through His death and resurrection.
Problems: Examples of sin, brokenness, hurt, failure, or any other problems that are solved only through Christ	*See Genesis 6:5.* The human heart is evil, and wickedness fills the earth. This problem can only be solved through Christ, who is able to transform the hearts of humanity.
Symbols: Images or actions that predict an aspect of Christ's person or work	*See Genesis 7:23.* Only those who entered the ark were saved from God's judgment, just like only those who are in Christ will be saved from eternal judgment.

WHAT TO LOOK FOR	EXAMPLE (FROM GENESIS 6–9)
Themes: Concepts that repeat throughout Scripture and find their resolution in Christ	*See Genesis 9:1–7.* In these verses, God makes a covenant with Noah and his family that resembles the covenant made with Adam and Eve in Genesis 1:28–30. Covenants—or God's promises to His people—are a theme throughout Scripture. Through Christ, God's new covenant is established; therefore, this theme is ultimately resolved through Him.
Promises: Specific words of God that offer assurance of His faithfulness and are fulfilled in Christ	*See Genesis 9:15–16.* God promises to remember His covenant with Noah and not destroy humanity again. This promise finds its fulfillment in the coming of Christ, who makes a way for humanity to be saved and redeemed.
People: Figures throughout Scripture who point to Christ—sometimes through their success and faithfulness but, more often, through their failure to live up to their calling, thus pointing to Christ's perfection	*See Genesis 6:9 and 9:18–27.* Noah was righteous, found favor with God, and walked with Him, and God used Noah to save his family. But Noah was not perfect, as evidenced by his sin after the flood in Genesis 9:18–27. Noah could not change his own heart or the hearts of the people. This points to humanity's need for a Savior. Thankfully, Jesus is a true and better Noah. He is able to deliver people from judgment and transform their hearts.
Predictions: Passages that speak about future events that find their ultimate fulfillment in Christ	Such predictions are found mostly in the prophetic books of the Old Testament, so there is not an example from Genesis 6–9. *Examples include: Isaiah 9:6, Hosea 1:11.*

The Attributes of God

Another way we can see Christ in all of Scripture is by identifying and studying the attributes of God. These are the traits that are true of God throughout all time and history. And because our God is a triune God—three in one—these attributes are true of all three members of the Trinity: Father, Son, and Holy Spirit. As you work through this study, you may find it helpful to bookmark this page and come back to it often as you seek to discover glimpses and echoes of Christ's character and work in every passage you study.

Eternal

God has no beginning and no end. He always was, always is, and always will be.

HAB. 1:12 / REV. 1:8 / IS. 41:4

Faithful

God is incapable of anything but fidelity. He is loyally devoted to His plan and purpose.

2 TIM. 2:13 / DEUT. 7:9 / HEB. 10:23

Good

God is pure; there is no defilement in Him. He is unable to sin, and all He does is good.

GEN. 1:31 / PS. 34:8 / PS. 107:1

Gracious

God is kind, giving us gifts and benefits we do not deserve.

2 KINGS 13:23 / PS. 145:8
IS. 30:18

Holy

God is undefiled and unable to be in the presence of defilement. He is sacred and set-apart.

REV. 4:8 / LEV. 19:2 / HAB. 1:13

Incomprehensible

God is high above and beyond human understanding. He is unable to be fully known.

PS. 145:3 / IS. 55:8–9
ROM. 11:33–36

Immutable

God does not change. He is the same yesterday, today, and tomorrow.

1 SAM. 15:29 / ROM. 11:29
JAMES 1:17

Infinite

God is limitless. He exhibits all of His attributes perfectly and boundlessly.

ROM. 11:33–36 / IS. 40:28
PS. 147:5

Jealous

God is desirous of receiving the praise and affection He rightly deserves.

EX. 20:5 / DEUT. 4:23–24
JOSH. 24:19

Just

God governs in perfect justice. He acts in accordance with justice. In Him, there is no wrongdoing or dishonesty.

IS. 61:8 / DEUT. 32:4 / PS. 146:7–9

Loving

God is eternally, enduringly, steadfastly loving and affectionate. He does not forsake or betray His covenant love.

JN. 3:16 / EPH. 2:4–5 / 1 JN. 4:16

Merciful

God is compassionate, withholding from us the wrath that we deserve.

TITUS 3:5 / PS. 25:10
LAM. 3:22–23

Omnipotent

God is all-powerful; His strength is unlimited.

MAT. 19:26 / JOB 42:1–2
JER. 32:27

Omnipresent

God is everywhere; His presence is near and permeating.

PROV. 15:3 / PS. 139:7–10
JER. 23:23–24

Omniscient

God is all-knowing; there is nothing unknown to Him.

PS. 147:4 / I JN. 3:20
HEB. 4:13

Patient

God is long-suffering and enduring. He gives ample opportunity for people to turn toward Him.

ROM. 2:4 / 2 PET. 3:9 / PS. 86:15

Self-Existent

God was not created but exists by His power alone.

PS. 90:1–2 / JN. 1:4 / JN. 5:26

Self-Sufficient

God has no needs and depends on nothing, but everything depends on God.

IS. 40:28–31 / ACTS 17:24–25
PHIL. 4:19

Sovereign

God governs over all things; He is in complete control.

COL. 1:17 / PS. 24:1–2
1 CHRON. 29:11–12

Truthful

God is our measurement of what is fact. By Him we are able to discern true and false.

JN. 3:33 / ROM. 1:25 / JN. 14:6

Wise

God is infinitely knowledgeable and is judicious with His knowledge.

IS. 46:9–10 / IS. 55:9 / PROV. 3:19

Wrathful

God stands in opposition to all that is evil. He enacts judgment according to His holiness, righteousness, and justice.

PS. 69:24 / JN. 3:36 / ROM. 1:18

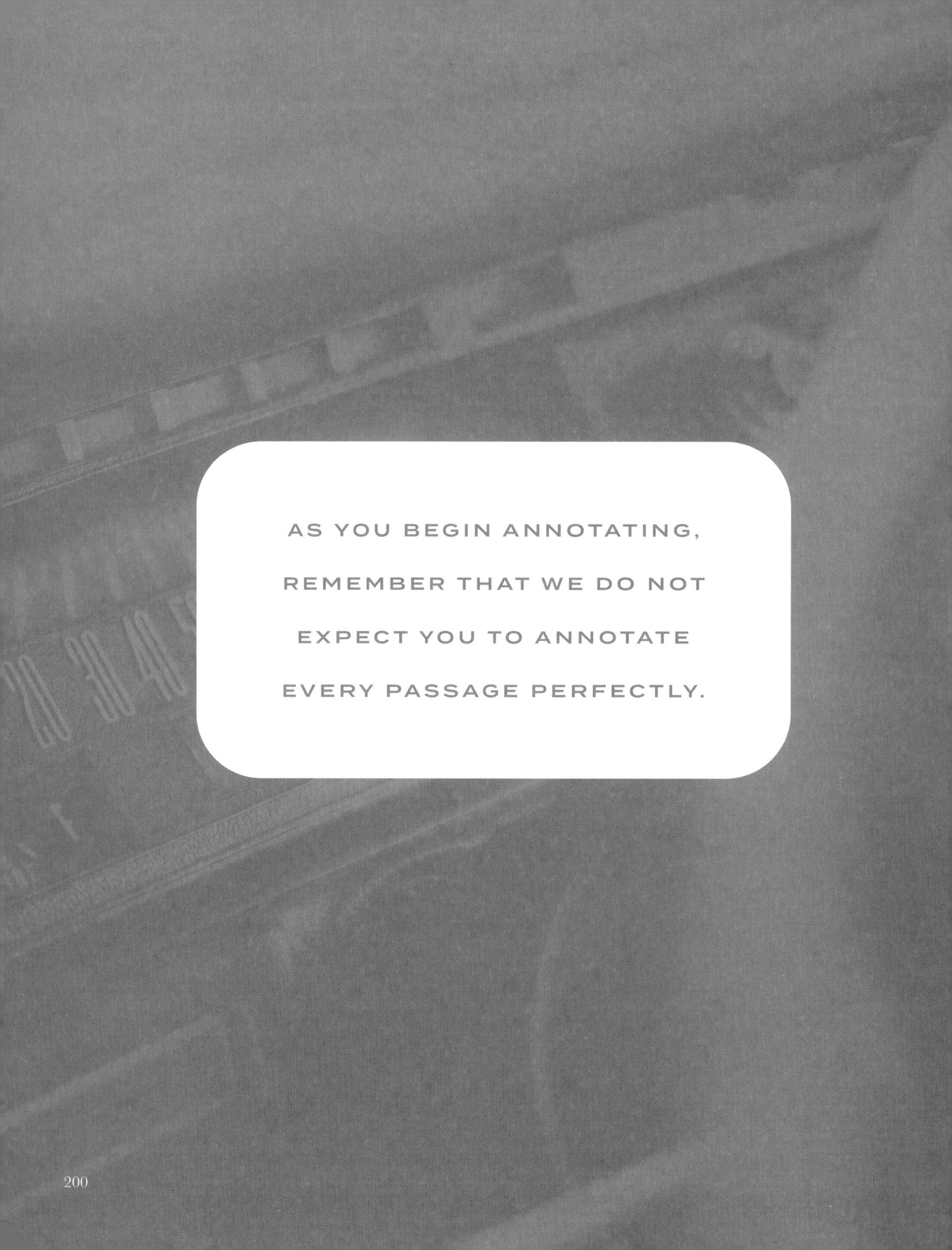

AS YOU BEGIN ANNOTATING, REMEMBER THAT WE DO NOT EXPECT YOU TO ANNOTATE EVERY PASSAGE PERFECTLY.

Annotation Examples and Tips

Each week of this study provides you with the opportunity to annotate two passages of Scripture—one from the Old Testament and one from the New Testament. In doing so, you will grow in your ability to study Scripture and make Christ connections in each passage you encounter. However, if the idea of annotation seems intimidating to you, do not fret! We have provided some helpful examples on the following pages, showing you what this might look like in a few different passages of Scripture.

As you begin annotating, remember that we do not expect you to annotate every passage perfectly. Additionally, if you come across an annotation prompt that challenges you or leaves you with more questions than answers, that's okay! You may find it helpful to look at the surrounding context of that passage (i.e., the verses or chapters that come just before and just after it). And at times, you may simply jot down your questions to come back to later in the week.

TIPS FOR ANNOTATING A PASSAGE

1. Look up key words in a concordance to identify cross-references.
2. Read the surrounding context of the passage (i.e., the verses or chapters that come before or after it) to aid your understanding.
3. As you look for connections to Jesus, use highlighters and/or write notes and questions in the margins.
4. If it is difficult to see the connection to Jesus, that is okay! Pray, read the verses surrounding the passage, and be patient as you read. Each week, the commentary will help you make those connections.

EXAMPLE ANNOTATION 1

PSALM 23 (THE GOOD SHEPHERD, A PSALM OF DAVID)

provider + protector
1 The LORD is my shepherd; I have what I need. 2 He lets
gracious
me lie down in green pastures; he leads me beside quiet
merciful *sovereign*
waters. 3 He renews my life; he leads me along the right
Holy
paths for his name's sake. 4 Even when I go through the
loving
darkest valley, I fear no danger, for you are with me; your
omnipotent + patient *gracious*
rod and your staff—they comfort me. 5 You prepare a table
before me in the presence of my enemies; you anoint my
good
head with oil; my cup overflows. 6 Only goodness and
faithful
faithful love will pursue me all the days of my life, and
omnipresent
I will dwell in the house of the LORD as long as I live.

PRAY, READ THE VERSES SURROUNDING THE PASSAGE, AND BE PATIENT AS YOU READ.

EXAMPLE ANNOTATION 2

PSALM 2 (CORONATION OF THE SON)

Problem (Rebellion)

1 Why do the nations rage and the peoples plot in vain?
2 The kings of the earth take their stand, and the
rulers conspire together against the Lord and his
Anointed One: 3 "Let's tear off their chains and throw
their ropes off of us." 4 The one enthroned in heaven
laughs; the Lord ridicules them. 5 Then he speaks
to them in his anger and terrifies them in his wrath:

People (King David)

6 "I have installed my king on Zion, my holy mountain."
7 I will declare the Lord's decree. He said to me,
"You are my Son; today I have become your Father.

↙

2 Samuel 7:14
Mark 1:11
Hebrews 1:5

Promise (Abrahamic covenant)

8 Ask of me, and I will make the nations your
inheritance and the ends of the earth your possession.
9 You will break them with an iron scepter; you
will shatter them like pottery." 10 So now, kings,
be wise; receive instruction, you judges of the
earth. 11 Serve the Lord with reverential awe
and rejoice with trembling. 12 Pay homage to
the Son or he will be angry and you will perish
in your rebellion, for his anger may ignite at any
moment. All who take refuge in him are happy.

In Christ, we find refuge.

EXAMPLE ANNOTATION 3

Titus 2:14
Hebrews 9:15

1 PETER 1:18–19

Promise (Redemption through faith in Jesus)

18 For you know that you were redeemed from

Problem (Sin)

your empty way of life inherited from your

Jesus's blood secures our redemption

ancestors, not with perishable things like silver

Theme (Sacrifice)

or gold, 19 but with the precious blood of Christ,

like that of an unblemished and spotless lamb.

Exodus 12
Isaiah 53:7
John 1:29

The Metanarrative of Scripture

In order to see Christ in all of Scripture, this study makes connections between the Old and New Testaments each week. In order to understand these connections, it is necessary to read the entire Bible through the lens of the metanarrative of Scripture—the four-part, overarching story of the Bible.

Creation

In the beginning, God created the universe. He made the world and everything in it. He created humans in His own image to be His representatives on the earth.

Fall

The first humans, Adam and Eve, disobeyed God by eating from the fruit of the Tree of the Knowledge of Good and Evil. Their disobedience impacted the whole world. The punishment for sin is death, and because of Adam's original sin, all humans are sinful and condemned to death.

Redemption

God sent His Son to become a human and redeem His people. Jesus Christ lived a sinless life but died on the cross to pay the penalty for sin. He resurrected from the dead and ascended into heaven. All who put their faith in Jesus are saved from death and freely receive the gift of eternal life.

Restoration

One day, Jesus Christ will return again and restore all that sin destroyed. He will usher in a new heaven and new earth where all who trust in Him will live eternally with glorified bodies in the presence of God.

WHAT IS THE GOSPEL?

Thank you for reading and enjoying this study with us! We are abundantly grateful for the Word of God, the instruction we glean from it, and the ever-growing understanding it provides for us of God's character. We are also thankful that Scripture continually points to one thing in innumerable ways: the gospel.

We remember our brokenness when we read about the fall of Adam and Eve in the garden of Eden (Genesis 3), where sin entered into a perfect world and maimed it. We remember the necessity that something innocent must die to pay for our sin when we read about the atoning sacrifices in the Old Testament. We read that we have all sinned and fallen short of the glory of God (Romans 3:23) and that the penalty for our brokenness, the wages of our sin, is death (Romans 6:23). We all need grace and mercy, but most importantly, we all need a Savior.

We consider the goodness of God when we realize that He did not plan to leave us in this dire state. We see His promise to buy us back from the clutches of sin and death in Genesis 3:15. And we see that promise accomplished with Jesus Christ on the cross. Jesus Christ knew no sin yet became sin so that we might become righteous through His sacrifice (2 Corinthians 5:21). Jesus was tempted in every way that we are and lived sinlessly. He was reviled yet still yielded Himself for our sake, that we may have life abundant in Him. Jesus lived the perfect life that we could not live and died the death that we deserved.

The gospel is profound yet simple. There are many mysteries in it that we will never understand this side of heaven, but there is still overwhelming weight to its implications in this life. The gospel tells of our sinfulness and God's goodness and a gracious gift that compels a response. We are saved by grace through faith, which means that we rest with faith in the grace that Jesus Christ displayed on the cross (Ephesians 2:8–9). We cannot save ourselves from our brokenness or do any amount of good works to merit God's favor. Still, we can have faith that what Jesus accomplished in His death, burial, and resurrection was more than enough for our salvation and our eternal delight. When we accept God, we are commanded to die to ourselves and our sinful desires and live a life worthy of the calling we have received (Ephesians 4:1). The gospel compels us to be sanctified, and in so doing, we are conformed to the likeness of Christ Himself. This is hope. This is redemption. This is the gospel.

SCRIPTURES TO REFERENCE

GENESIS 3:15

I will put hostility between you and the woman, and between your offspring and her offspring. He will strike your head, and you will strike his heel.

ROMANS 3:23

For all have sinned and fall short of the glory of God.

ROMANS 6:23

For the wages of sin is death, but the gift of God is eternal life in Christ Jesus our Lord.

2 CORINTHIANS 5:21

He made the one who did not know sin to be sin for us, so that in him we might become the righteousness of God.

EPHESIANS 2:8–9

For you are saved by grace through faith, and this is not from yourselves; it is God's gift—not from works, so that no one can boast.

EPHESIANS 4:1–3

Therefore I, the prisoner in the Lord, urge you to walk worthy of the calling you have received, with all humility and gentleness, with patience, bearing with one another in love, making every effort to keep the unity of the Spirit through the bond of peace.

BIBLIOGRAPHY

Athas, George. *Deuteronomy: One Nation under God.* Edited by Paul Barnett. Reading the Bible Today Series. Sydney, South NSW: Aquila Press, 2016.

Barclay, William. *The Letter to the Romans.* 3rd ed. The New Daily Study Bible. Louisville, KY: Westminster John Knox Press, 2002.

Blum, Edwin A., and Trevin Wax, eds. CSB Study Bible. Nashville, TN: Holman Bible Publishers, 2017.

Boa, Kenneth, and William Kruidenier. *Romans.* Holman New Testament Commentary. Nashville, TN: Broadman & Holman Publishers, 2000.

Carson, D. A., ed. *NIV Biblical Theology Study Bible.* Grand Rapids, MI: Zondervan, 2018.

Carson, D. A. *The Gospel according to John.* The Pillar New Testament Commentary. Grand Rapids, MI: William B. Eerdmans Publishing Company, 1991.

Douglas, J. D., and Merrill C. Tenney. *Zondervan Illustrated Bible Dictionary.* Revised by Moisés Silva. Grand Rapids, MI: Zondervan Academic, 2011.

Elwell, Walter A., ed. *Evangelical Commentary on the Bible.* Vol. 3. Grand Rapids, MI: Baker Book House, 1995.

Enns, Peter. *The NIV Application Commentary: Exodus.* Grand Rapids, MI: Zondervan, 2000.

Faithlife, LLC. "Blessings and Curses." Logos Bible Software, Computer software. Logos Bible Software Factbook. Bellingham, WA: Faithlife, LLC, November 11, 2023. https://ref.ly/logos4/Factbook?ref=bk.%25blessingsAndCurses.

Frame, John M. *Systematic Theology: An Introduction to Christian Belief.* Phillipsburg, NJ: P&R Publishing, 2013.

Gangel, Kenneth O. *John.* Holman New Testament Commentary. Nashville, TN: Broadman & Holman Publishers, 2000.

Greear, J. D., and Heath A. Thomas. *Exalting Jesus in 1 & 2 Samuel.* Christ-Centered Exposition Commentary. Nashville, TN: Holman Reference, 2016.

Green, Michael. *The Message of Matthew: The Kingdom of Heaven.* The Bible Speaks Today. Downers Grove, IL: InterVarsity Press, 2001.

Keener, Craig S. *The IVP Bible Background Commentary: New Testament.* 2nd ed. Downers Grove, IL: IVP Academic, 2014.

Kidner, Derek. *Ezra and Nehemiah: An Introduction and Commentary.* Vol. 12 of Tyndale Old Testament Commentaries. Downers Grove, IL: InterVarsity Press, 1979.

Liddell, Henry George, and Robert Scott. *An Intermediate Greek-English Lexicon: Founded Upon the Seventh Edition of Liddell and Scott's Greek-English Lexicon.* Mansfield Centre, CT: Martino Publishing, 2013.

Longman, Tremper, III. *How to Read Exodus.* Downers Grove, IL: IVP Academic, 2009.

Mackie, Tim. "What's the Meaning of the Jewish Shema Prayer in the Bible?" *The Bible Project.* May 26, 2017. https://bibleproject.com/articles/what-is-the-shema/.

Morris, Leon. *The Gospel according to John, Revised.* The New International Commentary on the New Testament. Grand Rapids, MI: William B. Eerdmans Publishing Company, 1995.

Moseley, Allan. *Exalting Jesus in Leviticus.* Christ-Centered Exposition Commentary. Nashville, TN: Holman Reference, 2015.

Pratt Jr., Richard L. *I & II Corinthians.* Holman New Testament Commentary. Nashville, TN: Broadman & Holman Publishers, 2000.

Stott, John R. W. *God's New Society: The Message of Ephesians.* The Bible Speaks Today. Downers Grove, IL: InterVarsity Press, 1979.

Stott, John R. W. *The Message of Romans: God's Good News for the World.* The Bible Speaks Today. Downers Grove, IL: InterVarsity Press, 2001.

Thompson, J. A. *Deuteronomy: An Introduction and Commentary.* Vol. 5 of Tyndale Old Testament Commentaries. Downers Grove, IL: InterVarsity Press, 1974.

Walvoord, John F., and Roy B. Zuck, ed. *The Bible Knowledge Commentary.* Wheaton, IL: Victor Books, 1985.

Youngblood, Ronald F., ed. *Nelson's New Illustrated Bible Dictionary.* Nashville, TN: Thomas Nelson, 1995.

OUR FAITH IS ANCHORED

IN GOD'S ABILITY

AND NOT OUR OWN.

INDEX

Old Testament

DEUTERONOMY

JOSHUA

JUDGES

RUTH

1 SAMUEL

2 SAMUEL

7:12–16 . . . . . 179, 180, 181, 186, 188

2 KINGS

1 CHRONICLES

PSALMS

New Testament

1 CORINTHIANS

2 CORINTHIANS

GALATIANS

EPHESIANS

PHILIPPIANS

COLOSSIANS

HEBREWS

1 PETER

1 JOHN

REVELATION

Thank you for studying God's Word with us!

CONNECT WITH US

@thedailygraceco

@dailygracepodcast

CONTACT US

info@thedailygraceco.com

SHARE

#thedailygraceco

VISIT US ONLINE

www.thedailygraceco.com

MORE DAILY GRACE

Daily Grace® Podcast